B R I S T O L

CITY·COAST·COUNTRYSIDE

This book is about the places that make Bristol special. It does not aim to be a detailed visitors' guide, but it will hopefully inspire people to explore Bristol and the surrounding area, whether they live in the city or come from far afield.

By any yardstick, Bristol is one of the great cities of Europe. The sheer variety and brilliance of its treasures will amply reward the effort of discovery.

TOP DETAIL: ST. PAUL'S FESTIVAL. MAIN PICTURE: LASER SHOW
IN BRISTOL HISTORIC HARBOUR.

TOP DETAIL: DRAWING BY NICHOLAS POCOCK FROM THE LOG OF
THE SHIP *LLOYD*, 1771–2. MAIN PICTURE: THE MENDIP HILLS.
BOTTOM DETAIL: THE WILDFOWL TRUST AT SLIMBRIDGE.

Further information about places of interest in and around Bristol, opening times, etc., is available from your local Tourist Information Centre.

Produced and published by Bristol City Council © 1989.

Design and concept by the Exhibition and Graphic Design Section of the City Planning Department.

Edited by the Press and Public Relations Office.

Written for the City Council by Sara Davies.

Printed by the Printing and Stationery Department.

ISBN 0 946506 21 3

Contents

Historic City Centre

Bristol grew from a Saxon settlement at the point where the River Frome joins the River Avon, and was well established by the eleventh century. Traders flourished in the shadow of the now-vanished castle, and the area remains the commercial heart of the city. Banking halls, offices and markets rub shoulders with places of worship and the green oases of city parks. Nearby Broadmead is the region's prime shopping centre. It was created out of the devastation of the Second World War and is still the subject of a steady programme of improvement and expansion.

CORN STREET

Corn Street has been at the active heart of Bristol ever since medieval times. The crossroads formed with Broad Street, Wine Street and High Street was the centre of the medieval city, where the Bristol High Cross once stood.

In the eighteenth century, Corn Street became the commercial centre of the city, and a series of imposing banking halls and business premises marked the city's prosperity. Although some buildings were destroyed by bombs in the Second World War, there still remain many splendid examples of the commercial wealth and architectural ambition of the city in the eighteenth and nineteenth centuries.

Notable are the Commercial Rooms, opened in 1811; the old Council House, at the top of the street; and Victorian architect W. B. Gingell's exuberant designs for what are now the Lloyds and National Westminster banks.

THE DUTCH HOUSE

One of the landmarks of old Bristol, destroyed by bombs in 1940, was the Dutch House, so called because it was believed, wrongly, to have been built out of materials from Holland. It stood on the corner of the main intersection of the city at Wine Street and High Street, and was one of the most splendid examples of timber-frame building left in Bristol. Said to date from 1676, it was unusual in having two timber-decorated façades, and in its height—five storeys plus attics and cellars. It was a *tour de force* of construction in an era when wood was the most practical building material available.

HIGH CROSS

The High Cross stood for over three centuries at the very centre of medieval Bristol on the crossroads formed by Corn Street, Wine Street, Broad Street and High Street. Commemorating Edward III's charter of 1373 granting county status to the town, it was brightly painted and decorated with four statues of medieval kings.

In 1733 it was removed at the request of local residents, who found it a 'ruinous and superstitious relick' and a public obstruction. For a few years it stood on College Green, but was once more removed when it was found to obstruct ladies and gentlemen walking on the green. It was then taken to the gardens at Stourhead in Wiltshire, where it has remained in safety and splendour without obstructing anyone ever since. A replica of the upper section of the Cross stands in the gardens of Berkeley Square, off Park Street.

TOP: THE TOWER OF ALL SAINTS' CHURCH RISES ABOVE CORN STREET AND CARWARDINE'S COFFEE HOUSE. LEFT: THE DUTCH HOUSE; RIGHT: EARLY DRAWING OF THE HIGH CROSS.

CHRISTCHURCH

The original church on this site was demolished in 1786—its fabric having decayed, like many medieval churches. The poet Robert Southey, who was born in nearby Wine Street, was baptised in the old parish church. The new church was built by William Paty, who was only 28 at the time, and consecrated in 1790. The colourful quarterjacks on the outside wall were designed by his grandfather earlier that century for the previous church, and still strike each quarter-hour.

ABOVE: THE QUARTER-JACKS OUTSIDE CHRISTCHURCH. BELOW: ALL SAINTS' CHURCH AND LEFT: A DETAIL FROM THE TOMB OF COLSTON BY RYSBRACK.

ALL SAINTS' CHURCH

The Church of All Saints is of Norman foundation, its twelfth-century origin visible in some of the pillars in the nave. In 1216 the church was assigned to the use of the Guild of Kalendars, an ancient fraternity whose chief function was to keep the records of the town. In 1451 the guild built a library in the church, said to have been the first free library in England, and certainly the first library in Bristol. Later burnt down, the library stood on the site now occupied by Carwardine's coffee shop.

The very fine church tower was completed in 1716 and repaired, with the addition of the cupola, in 1807. One of the contributors to the cost of the tower was Edward Colston, whose superb tomb is in the church. The effigy on it is an outstanding artistic achievement by the then unknown sculptor Rysbrack.

The church is still used for worship, but is also a very lively urban studies centre and frequently houses exhibitions of general interest.

CORN EXCHANGE AND NAILS

The Exchange is generally regarded as Bristol's finest Georgian public building. It was designed as a meeting place for the city's merchants and shipowners by celebrated Bath architect John Wood the Elder, after the model of the Royal Exchange in London. It opened in 1743, and from 1813 the city's twice-weekly corn markets were held in the building. It is now part of St. Nicholas' Markets, and an excellent place to browse for antiques and gifts.

On the pavement outside the Exchange are the Nails—four engraved bronze pillars dating from the sixteenth and seventeenth centuries. These originally stood in an arcade nearby called the Merchants' Tolzey, and served as trading tables where financial deals were struck—which may well have given rise to the expression 'to pay on the nail'.

TOP: THE CORN EXCHANGE. LEFT: ONE OF THE FAMOUS NAILS. BEHIND IS THE SUPERB MID-VICTORIAN LLOYDS BANK BUILDING IN SIXTEENTH-CENTURY VENETIAN STYLE. BELOW: THE RUMMER, NOW VIRTUALLY CONTAINED WITHIN THE GLASS-ROOFED MARKET.

THE RUMMER

The Rummer pub and restaurant stands on the site of the oldest inn in Bristol, the Green Lattis, believed to have been a public house as early as the thirteenth century.

It was demolished and rebuilt in the 1740s when the site was cleared for the Exchange, and, despite internal alterations and war damage, its exterior has not much changed since then. Several British monarchs have stayed in its rooms, and it was the point of arrival for the very first mail coach from London to Bristol in 1784.

ST. NICHOLAS' MARKETS

The glass-roofed market between the Exchange and High Street was built in 1745 as a way of relieving the congestion of stalls in the narrow streets of the city centre. Originally just for the sale of fruit and vegetables, the market has grown over the years to include a fish-market, flowerstalls, wholefoods, bric-à-brac and second-hand books. Now the biggest and most varied indoor market complex in the West Country, St. Nicholas' includes two floors in the Corn Exchange, where antiques and second-hand goods are sold.

TOP: VICTORIAN DRINKING-FOUNTAIN SITUATED JUST OUTSIDE THE MARKET. THE MARKET ITSELF (OTHER PICTURES) BOASTS A WIDE RANGE OF DIFFERENT MERCHANDISE.

ST. NICHOLAS' CHURCH MUSEUM

The medieval church of St. Nicholas was part of the city wall, whose main gate to the south, across Bristol Bridge, ran beneath the church's chancel. In the mid-eighteenth century this upper church and gateway were replaced by the light-filled Georgian-Gothic space of today. The very beautiful crypt, dating from 1375–1400, was left intact, and now houses a popular brass-rubbing centre.

A balcony and stage were added to the nave when the church became a museum and performance space in 1973, and a late eighteenth-century chamber organ by Sarah Green of London was restored for recitals and accompaniment. The nave now displays a selection of church plate and other treasures from the diocese of Bristol, while the city's early history is exhibited on the balcony. Beneath, in an area protected from daylight, is a changing selection from the museum's unique collection of drawings and watercolours of Bristol life before its Victorian development.

The whole upper church is dominated by William Hogarth's enormous triptych, painted for St. Mary Redcliffe in 1755/6. This never found a comfortable home until cleaned and set-up in St. Nicholas', within its re-gilded frame, in 1973.

ABOVE: DETAIL FROM THE LARGE-SCALE HOGARTH PAINTING.

ABOVE: THE POPULAR BRASS RUBBING CENTRE IN THE CRYPT OF ST. NICHOLAS' CHURCH MUSEUM.

BROAD STREET

Broad Street was one of medieval Bristol's main streets. For almost 700 years the legal business of the city was carried out from the Guildhall, and it was here that Judge Jeffreys held his 'Bloody Assize' after the Monmouth Rebellion in 1685. In 1843 a new Guildhall was built by Bristol architect Pope. The Bank of England, designed by Cockerell in 1846, is an impressive triumph of Victorian architecture, while the façade of Edward Everard's printing house near the bottom of the street, all tiled in Carrara marble, is a masterpiece of art nouveau decoration. Two famous old inns, the White Lion and the White Hart, were rebuilt in the 1860s to create the Grand Hotel, providing more luxurious accommodation for prosperous visitors to the city.

ABOVE: THE ART NOUVEAU FAÇADE OF THE EDWARD EVERARD BUILDING IN BROAD STREET. LEFT: THIS SUPERB SHELL HOOD CAN BE FOUND OVER THE DOOR OF THE MERCHANT TAILORS' HALL IN NEARBY TAILORS' COURT. RIGHT: THE GRAND HOTEL.

BOVE: AN ARCHIVE PHOTOGRAPH SHOWS BROAD STREET IN THE VICTORIAN PERIOD.

ST. JOHN'S CHURCH AND GATE

The fourteenth-century church of St. John the Baptist was one of four churches built on the old wall which once fortified the Norman town of Bristol. Only two now remain, St. John's and St. Nicholas', and both have vaulted crypts underneath—now rarely found anywhere in the country. St. John's is unique in the city in that its tower and spire, originally shared with another church on the wall immediately to the west, are built over the only medieval gateway into the city still in existence. The outline of the original door to the church is still clearly visible in the eastern wall of the main arch. The interior of the church is unaisled and most attractive in its simplicity, as is the crypt below it.

The vaulted arch of St. John's gateway bears the figures of Brennus and Belinus, the legendary founders of Bristol, sitting in niches at either side. The groove in the gate which would once have taken the portcullis can be clearly seen.

The cemetery for St. John's Church, at the end of Tailors' Court off Broad Street, is at some distance from the church itself.

ST. JOHN'S CONDUIT

In 1267 the order of the Carmelite Friars decided to pipe water to the friary from their spring on Brandon Hill. In 1376 they agreed to supply a 'feather' or branch pipe to the parishioners of St. John's on the Wall.

The conduit they installed has been a source of water for the subsequent 600 years, and a plaque records that for a short time during the Second World War it was the only supply of water to the blitzed centre of the city.

LEFT: ST. JOHN'S CONDUIT. RIGHT: ST. JOHN'S CHURCH AND GATE. CENTRE: A DETAIL FROM THE PAINTED CARVINGS ON THE ARCH.

13

BRISTOL CASTLE

Although no longer visible (it was almost all demolished by Act of Parliament in 1650), the site of Bristol Castle can still be made out in Castle Park between the Holiday Inn and the ruins of St. Peter's Church. The castle, founded before 1088, was walled and contained within it an enormous stone keep 90 feet or more square with corner turrets. At the west end lay the king's hall and private quarters where the business of the realm was carried on during the monarch's visit. Of this complex only the twin porches which formed the entrance are still standing, but these do contain traces of the fine architecture which characterised royal buildings in the Middle Ages. At the west end, near St. Peter's Church, can be seen a sally-port in the form of a rock-cut tunnel with several steps. This was used during sieges to send troops to attack sappers whose task was to undermine the walls of the castle. There are plans to improve the interpretation of this important royal fortress with a general enhancement of Castle Park.

BROADMEAD

This part of the city was badly bombed during the Second World War, and now bears few traces of its pre-war existence apart from a few isolated buildings. After the war it was developed as the main shopping area for the city, and, although rather a dismal reflection on post-war urban architecture, is an excellent retail centre serving Bristol and the region. Branches of all the main department and chain stores as well as many smaller specialist shops are conveniently located in a largely pedestrianised area, which has recently been much improved by the City Council's addition of brick paving, seating and trees. Plans are in hand to upgrade the shopping facilities further, and to extend Broadmead so that it remains the region's prime retail area.

At one end of Broadmead is the Horsefair, for over 500 years the site of the famous eight-day St. James Fair, last held in 1838.

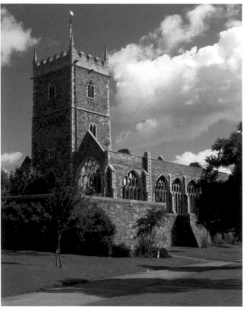

DETAIL RIGHT: THE CITY'S MEDIEVAL SEAL SHOWING THE CASTLE. TOP: A RE-CREATION BY THE CITY MUSEUM AND ART GALLERY OF BRISTOL CASTLE. BOTTOM LEFT: PART OF THE MOAT STILL SURVIVES. BOTTOM RIGHT: THE SHELL OF THE FOURTEENTH-CENTURY ST. PETER'S CHURCH IS PRESERVED AS A REMINDER OF THE SECOND WORLD WAR.

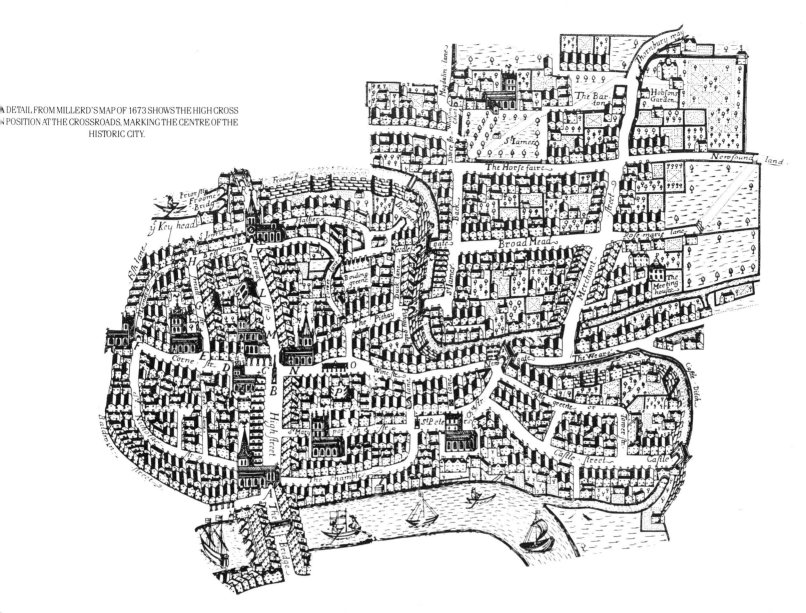

A DETAIL FROM MILLERD'S MAP OF 1673 SHOWS THE HIGH CROSS IN POSITION AT THE CROSSROADS, MARKING THE CENTRE OF THE HISTORIC CITY.

LEFT: THE ARCADE SURVIVED THE SECOND WORLD WAR, BUT MOST OF BROADMEAD (RIGHT) HAS BEEN DEVELOPED SINCE.

THE NEW ROOM AND WESLEY

The New Room, another relic of old Bristol in the centre of Broadmead, marks the strong association the city has long had with English Nonconformism. The first Methodist chapel in the country, it was built by John Wesley in 1739 to provide a place of worship for the

increasing number of Methodists in the city. Methodist preachers were excluded from most established churches, and their followers were forced to meet in small groups or attend the large, open-air gatherings addressed by evangelists like Wesley and George Whitefield.

The site chosen by Wesley for his New Room was a small plot near the Horsefair, on which was built a narrow, two-tiered chapel with small living quarters for the preacher on top. The design is unusual, and attractive in its simplicity, reflecting the Methodists' rejection of the high ornamentation favoured by the established church of the time. There is a particularly interesting double pulpit from which Wesley himself preached many times during his frequent visits to the city.

Outside in the courtyard is a fine bronze equestrian statue of Wesley, and behind the building is another of his brother Charles, who lived in the city until 1779.

QUAKERS' FRIARS

Quakers' Friars is an extraordinary oasis of old Bristol tucked away in the heart of the modern shopping centre. The buildings were originally part of the cloisters of the Dominican friary built on this site—one of five friaries in medieval Bristol, the other four of which have completely disappeared.

During the seventeenth century a part of the cloisters was bought by the Quaker Society of Friends as a meeting house. The interior has been largely rebuilt over the centuries, but the exterior has changed little.

Many of Bristol's leading trading families have been Quakers, and the city had strong connections with the early evangelists of the movement. George Fox, its founder, was married at Quakers' Friars in 1669, as was William Penn, another Quaker leader and the founder of the state of Pennsylvania in the United States. He married his second wife, Hannah Callowhill, the

daughter of a well-to-do Bristol linen draper, at t[?] Friars in 1696. He had moved to Bristol the previo[?] year after setting up his new colony in America, a[?] stayed in the city for the next three years.

Quakers' Friars is now Bristol's Central Regist[?] Office, and used for all the civil marriages that take pla[?] in the city.

ST. JAMES' CHURCH

The West End of St. James' Church near the Haymarket is believed to be the oldest surviving structure in Bristol. It was a church for the Benedictine priory founded by Robert, Earl of Gloucester, in 1120, when Bristol's importance was increasing and he was also building the Great Keep of Bristol Castle. He set aside every tenth stone from the castle to build the Lady Chapel at St. James'. Among other twelfth-century detail is an early example of a 'wheel window' in the nave.

ST. JAMES' PARK

This former churchyard is a popular lunchtime haven for workers from the busy city centre shops and offices on summer days. It was already a city centre park before heavy bombing in the Second World War devastated Broadmead, and after the war was one of the first areas to be reconstructed.

TOP: THE TRANQUILLITY OF ST. JAMES' PARK, OVERLOOKED BY ST. JAMES' CHURCH. BOTTOM: THE DRAMATIC NEW SPECTRUM BUILDING.

The Centre and
College Green

Few areas of Bristol have changed over the centuries as dramatically as the Centre. Parts of it have been land, then water, then land again—not through accidents of nature but as a result of deliberate planning on a grand scale.

A casual glance may reveal no more than a tide of cars and people flowing between high buildings devoted to business, entertainment and worship. But look a little closer . . . some of those buildings are very fine; the cityscape is softened by water and greenery; and a sense of history survives amid the bustle of modern city life.

THE CENTRE

The area known as the Centre of Bristol is a fairly recent development in the city's landscape.

Once an area of marshy ground skirting the western side of the Anglo-Saxon city, this land was excavated in the thirteenth century in order to divert the River Frome and construct an improved harbour for the rapidly expanding port. The dockside thus created once extended at least as far as the point where Electricity House now stands. Photographs of the Centre in the nineteenth century show a bustling quayside scene, crowded with the masts of tall ships and trading vessels from all over the world.

Between 1898 and 1938 this arm of the harbour was progressively covered over to form the gardens and road network of the Centre as it now exists.

THE QUAYHEAD

At one end of the Centre is the quayhead, marking the point at which the River Frome now disappears underground. Here in the small garden stands the lead-cast statue of Neptune, originally erected in 1792 by Joseph Rendall in the Temple area of the city and then moved to its present, appropriate spot in 1949.

Next to the statue are three plaques commemorating the foremost of the great seafarers whose names are associated with Bristol: John Cabot, who left from these docks in 1497 on his quest for mainland America; Captain Thomas James, a Bristolian who played an important role in the history of Ontario; and Samuel Plimsoll, also a Bristolian, who gave his name to the painted safety line around the hull of merchant ships.

This is the starting point for the Bristol Heritage Walk. This circular route of 2¾ miles (4.5 km) is an ideal introduction to the historic centre of the city, and is easily followed by the pavement markings. Guide books are obtainable from the Tourist Information Centre and most bookshops.

TOP: BROAD QUAY IN 1735. THIS VIEW TOWARDS ST. MICHAEL'S HILL SHOWS WHAT IS NOW THE CENTRE. LEFT: STATUE OF NEPTUNE. BOTTOM: THE CENTRE IN THE VICTORIAN PERIOD.

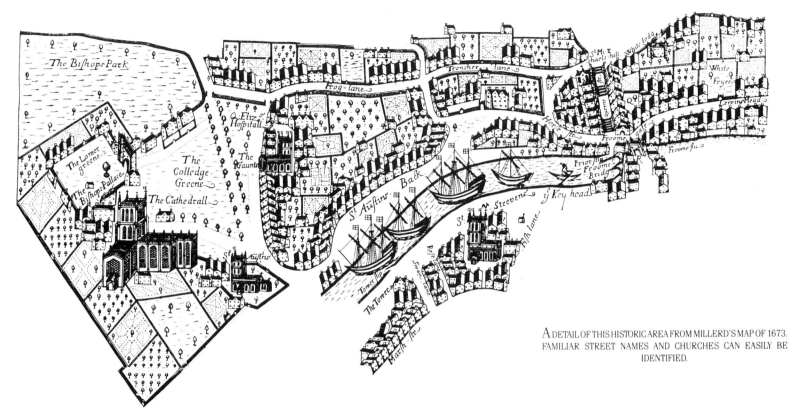

A DETAIL OF THIS HISTORIC AREA FROM MILLERD'S MAP OF 1673. FAMILIAR STREET NAMES AND CHURCHES CAN EASILY BE IDENTIFIED.

THE CENTRE GARDENS ARE WELL MAINTAINED BY THE CITY COUNCIL'S PARKS DEPARTMENT.

ABOVE: ORIGINALLY THE TRAMWAYS CENTRE, NOW OFFICES AND SHOPS. BELOW: A PARADE OF SPECTACULAR ILLUMINATED FLOATS CELEBRATES THE SWITCHING ON OF THE CHRISTMAS LIGHTS.

TRAMWAYS CENTRE

A number of half-timbered houses along the old quayside on St. Augustine's Parade, dating from the mid seventeenth century onwards, were progressively taken over in the 1920s by the Bristol Omnibus Company for their offices. They were considerably rebuilt inside and decorated with the historically anachronistic but charming half-timbered ornamentation which, together with the clock, became a popular feature of the city centre.

Recent renovation work on the buildings, instigated by Bristol City Council, has restored much of their historical authenticity whilst allowing development of the shop and office space appropriate to the area.

EDMUND BURKE

Dublin-born politician Edmund Burke was Member of Parliament for Bristol from 1774 to 1780. He was an exceptional orator and writer, who spoke eloquently against the war with the American colonies and in support of Catholic emancipation. He was one of the principal and most articulate champions of William Wilberforce's campaign to abolish the slave trade.

In later life he became estranged from his earlier progressive associates, delivered a nine-day speech urging the impeachment of Bengal's Governor-General Warren Hastings, and crossed the floor of the House of Commons to sit next to his old enemy Pitt.

His bronze statue in the city centre (pictured below) is a replica of the marble one in St. Stephen's Hall, Westminster. A copy was presented to America and unveiled in Washington in 1922.

EDWARD COLSTON

One of the great benefactors of Bristol, Edward Colston was born in Temple Street in 1636, the eldest son of merchant William Colston. He inherited his father's business in 1681, and, although he did not live in the city, it was to Bristol that he gave much of his wealth.

He was a shrewd and hard-headed businessman who, whilst undoubtedly philanthropic, was described in many contemporary accounts as a difficult and bigoted man, not averse to using his wealth and patronage against the city corporation (the forerunner of Bristol City Council) if necessary.

He founded an almshouse on St. Michael's Hill and paid for the enlargement of the seamen's almshouses in King Street. He was particularly concerned about the education of the poor, and founded and endowed a new school—Colston's Boys' School—which still exists.

He was a committed Tory and churchman, and at the age of 74 was elected Member of Parliament for Bristol, although he retired three years later.

By the time he died in 1721 he had distributed over £70,000 publicly as well as large sums privately. Bristol still bears many reminders of his patronage, and various societies continue his charitable work to this day.

ST. MARY ON THE QUAY

As its name implies, this imposing chapel originally stood on the waterfront. It was commissioned in 1839 by the followers of evangelist Henry Irving from distinguished architect Richard Shackleton Pope, who designed it with a temple front in the Corinthian style much admired at the time. The Irvingites, however, did not flourish, and when the chapel was abandoned four years later it was taken over by Bishop Baines, a passionate devotee of the Grecian style, as the centre of Catholic worship in the city.

ABOVE: ST. MARY ON THE QUAY. MAIN PICTURE: THE STATUE OF EDWARD COLSTON ON THE CENTRE.

COLSTON HALL

The Colston Hall is the region's major concert hall, and offers a very varied programme of entertainment from symphony and rock concerts to wrestling. It hosts the Bournemouth Symphony Orchestra season from October to May, and frequent BBC radio broadcasts, as well as the televised award ceremonies for the 'Sci-Tech' and 'Wildscreen' festivals held in the city.

The building, which opened in 1867, has changed little externally, but has twice been rebuilt inside after fire damage—first in 1898 and again in 1945.

HIPPODROME

The Bristol Hippodrome was opened in December 1912, part of the growing theatre empire of impresario Oswald Stoll. It was designed by Frank Matcham, the greatest theatre architect of his day. It was built on what was at that time the quayside and a maritime theme ran throughout the decor of the building, but its most sensational feature was its stage. This was made in four independently operated sections with a huge water tank underneath, making spectacular effects such as tidal waves and waterfalls possible.

Until 1964, when it was removed in modernisation work together with the tower and top storey, a revolving globe topped the Hippodrome, echoing the one which still exists (though no longer revolves) on the London Coliseum. Still surviving, however, is the dome in the roof above the stalls, which slides open to reveal the stars on particularly sultry nights.

After a rather rocky period in the 1960s and 1970s, the Hippodrome has gone from strength to strength in the 1980s, reaffirming its place as the West Country's premier large-scale stage, ideal for the musicals, opera and ballet that regularly bring in capacity audiences.

TOP: PEKING ACROBATS ON TOUR PERFORM AT THE COLSTON HALL. TOP RIGHT: COLSTON HALL. BOTTOM: AUDITORIUM OF THE HIPPODROME. THE DOME HAS BEEN OPENED TO ALLOW IN FRESH AIR AND DAYLIGHT.

CHRISTMAS STEPS

Once a muddy lane known as Steep Street, leading up from the Frome Bridge outside the city walls of medieval Bristol, the picturesque street now called Christmas Steps was probably little more than a haunt for footpads and amorous couples until the middle of the seventeenth century.

In September 1669, as an inscription at the top of the steps tells us, it was 'stepper'd, done and finished' at the personal expense of Jonathan Blackwell, a wealthy wine merchant who had been Sheriff of Bristol.

At this time the steps led out of the complex of lanes around Host Street to what was rapidly becoming a residential neighbourhood at the top of St. Michael's Hill. There are no sixteenth- or seventeeth-century houses surviving today on Christmas Steps. The oldest date from the eighteenth century—at least externally, although there are likely to be fascinating earlier features inside many of them.

The character of the steps is, however, remarkably close to what it must have been in medieval times, not least because of an imaginative piece of architectural recreation at the foot of the hill. In the 1960s the buildings here were demolished to make way for the widening of the Inner Circuit Road, thus leaving the bottom of the steps exposed to the rush of city traffic. In the 1970s the City Council's planners decided to try to repair the damage, and the bottom of the steps was closed off once more by the re-creation of a network of intricate spaces. Here a combination of careful new construction and restoration work on existing seventeenth- and eighteenth-century buildings like the popular Victorian fish and chip shop has given back to Christmas Steps its unique appeal.

ST. BARTHOLEMEW'S

At the foot of Christmas Steps is a porchway, a rare survival of medieval Bristol and all that remains of the Hospital of St. Bartholemew's.

Founded in the thirteenth century as an almshouse for the poor and sick, it stood just outside the walls of the original town, on the north bank of the River Frome. In 1532 the Bristol Grammar School was established in the, by then decaying, buildings. Inside, several surviving sections of the original hospital can still be seen. Recent restoration around the porch has helped bring back to this corner of Bristol some of the flavour of the timber-frame buildings which would have characterised the city in the seventeenth century.

TOP LEFT: CHRISTMAS STEPS IN THE VICTORIAN PERIOD AND (TOP RIGHT) TODAY. ABOVE: AT THE BOTTOM OF THE STEPS THE MEDIEVAL STREET PATTERN HAS BEEN RESTORED.

25

FOSTER'S ALMSHOUSE

At the top of Christmas Steps is Foster's Almshouse and the tiny Chapel of the Three Kings of Cologne. Both were founded by John Foster, a wealthy Bristol merchant who

was Sheriff of the City in 1474, Mayor in 1481 and Member of Parliament in 1489.

The almshouse was built first, in 1481, the chapel in 1484. The dedication to the three kings is believed to be unique in Britain, and is likely to be the result of John Foster's journeys as a trader in the Rhineland, where he would have seen and been impressed by the Chapel of the Three Kings in Cologne Cathedral.

Both almshouse and chapel were renovated several times over the centuries in keeping with the architectural fashions of the period. The almshouse underwent major changes in the nineteenth century, when it was enlarged and rebuilt in the Burgundian Gothic style by a well-known Bristol architect also called, coincidentally, John Foster.

Final restoration of the almshouse and chapel was completed in the 1960s, and included the carving of the three kings on the front of the chapel by Bristol artist Ernest Pascoe. Today these striking Gothic surroundings provide up-to-date accommodation for 26 residents.

ST. STEPHEN'S CHURCH

The parish of St. Stephen was established in the thirteenth century, but nothing remains of the first parish church except some traces inside the present building, which dates from the late fifteenth century.

The finest of Bristol's late medieval churches, its construction reflected the needs of the merchant community for whom it was built. Aisled, with no chancel arch or transepts, it had as many as nine separate chapel altars, where chaplains would sing private masses on behalf of individuals or families.

During the Reformation these altars were destroyed.

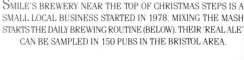

Even greater damage, however, was wreaked by the great storm of November 1703, said to have been one of the worst hurricanes to hit Northern Europe. Major reconstruction was necessary after this disaster, but it was not until 1875 that real restoration was undertaken, resulting in a thorough 're-Gothicisation' of the church according to the taste of the time. This work was made possible by the Antient Society of St. Stephen's Ringers, who embarked enthusiastically on the task of raising money for the church over the next 50 years.

Their greatest achievement was the re-facing of the splendid south-western tower. This was originally erected in 1470 at the expense of wealthy merchant and Mayor of Bristol, John Shipward. In four stages, topped by intricately worked pinnacles, it is one of the finest features in central Bristol.

Next to the tower is the South Porch, distinguished by its beautiful fan vaulting and rich panelling.

Inside the church are several notable monuments, including the tomb of fourteenth-century cloth merchant Edmund Blanket—who is unlikely, contrary to popular myth, to have given his name to the bed-cover, but who may have taken it from the fabric 'blanquette' in which he traded. The monument to Martin Pring, sea captain and discoverer of Cape Cod Bay, is also splendid, as is the imposing Jacobean tomb of Mr Justice Snygge, with its garbled Latin inscription, clearly too much for the local engraver to cope with.

TOP: FOSTER'S ALMSHOUSE. LEFT: ST. STEPHEN'S CHURCH. ABOVE: DETAIL FROM THE MONUMENT TO BRISTOL SEAFARER AND EXPLORER MARTIN PRING.

LEWIN'S MEAD CHAPEL

This is one of the finest surviving Nonconformist chapels in the country. It stands on the site of the medieval Frome Bridge, and was built in 1787 for the wealthy Unitarian Free Church of Lewin's Mead, who were dissatisfied with the modest chapel that had stood on the site since 1694. Additional land was purchased to build not only a larger meeting house but also a mews at the back for the many coaches in which families came from the city suburbs.

Used as a place of worship until 1985, but periodically threatened with demolition, Lewin's Mead was bought in 1986 by the Business Design Group and converted into a design studio and showroom. Care was taken to respect the original open, simple proportions of the interior and the attractive façade, thus preserving for Bristol one of its important city centre features. The building is open to the public at certain times of the year.

ABOVE: SPLENDID INTERIOR OF LEWIN'S MEAD CHAPEL, NOW CONVERTED TO OFFICE USE. LEFT: HEADQUARTERS OF THE BRISTOL AND WEST BUILDING SOCIETY.

COLLEGE GREEN

Dominated by the two imposing buildings of the Cathedral and the Council House, the triangular lawns of College Green were once the burial grounds of the medieval abbey and are now the focus for many public entertainments and events.

The short hill down from the Green represents the original slope of the bank to the river, and the steps at one corner once led directly onto the quayside. The statue of Queen Victoria in this corner was erected as a memorial of her Golden Jubilee in 1887, and unveiled by her son Prince Albert Victor in 1888.

THE COUNCIL HOUSE

For many centuries, Bristol's municipal administration was carried out from Corn Street, where three successive Council Houses were built over the years. With the expansion of local government in the twentieth century, it was decided to build new and larger premises on College Green.

The foundation stone for the new Council House, designed by architect Vincent Harris, was laid in 1938. Work on the building was delayed by the outbreak of war the following year, and it was not until several years after the war, when the economic climate improved

TOP: STATUE OF QUEEN VICTORIA. MAIN PICTURE: THE COUNCIL HOUSE AND COLLEGE GREEN. BOTTOM: AN EARLY DRAWING OF COLLEGE GREEN.

The ceremonial entrance leads into the main hall, paved in Belgian black marble and Bianco del Mar. Facing the entrance, and over the doorway to the Conference Hall, is a very fine blue and gold clock surrounded by the signs of the zodiac and equipped with a wind indicator. Cut into the stone walls of the Conference Hall are the names and dates of all the mayors and lord mayors of Bristol since 1216. The ceiling of the hall—the work of Tom Monnington—is one of the largest painted ceilings in the country, and its geometrical design was inspired by the symbols of atomic physics.

The Council House is the home of the city's municipal treasures. The Lord Mayor's Parlour houses the civic insignia, chief among which are four ceremonial swords: the Mourning Sword, dating from about 1373; the Pearl Sword from the late fourteenth century; the Lent Sword from the fifteenth century and the eighteenth-century State Sword. The eight silver maces are now carried in procession by police officers and the City Treasurer has a seventeenth-century copper gilt mace. Four Tudor silver chains, two silver trumpets and a silver oar—once carried by the water bailiff—complete the main items of Bristol's civic treasure.

sufficiently, that building was resumed. It was finished in 1953 and officially opened by Her Majesty Queen Elizabeth in 1956.

It is the largest example of 1930s neo-Georgian architecture in the city. Feelings about its style have been mixed: it has been criticised for lacking architectural imagination, like much twentieth-century municipal architecture, but on the other hand was faintly praised by architectural writer Nikolaus Pevsner as 'having more character than similar traditional buildings in other English cities'.

The adjoining Council Chamber also has a very fine ceiling, by John Armstrong and Mary Collett, on the theme of Bristol throughout its history. Both ceilings were gifts of the Edwin Austin Memorial Fund.

Set apart from these two large halls is the Civic Suite which comprises Committee Rooms, the Lord Mayor's Parlour and Reception Room, the Lady Mayoress' Parlour, a sitting room for women councillors and a retiring room.

Set in a graceful curve with pavilion entrances at either end, it forms an imposing crescent-shaped base to the gardens of College Green. A ceremonial approach-road sweeps up the curve of the crescent to a central entrance, above which is an archway carrying a symbolic figure of an Elizabethan seaman, marking the city's long association with seafaring exploration and trade. At each end of the steeply-sloping roof is a bronze-gilt unicorn bearing the city arms. The rear roof of the building is decorated with two finials consisting of a seahorse and the figures of a boy and girl, to represent the spirit of the Avon as a symbol of belief in the future of the city.

Among the offices in the Council House is the Bristol Record Office, which looks after the city's historical archives and the City Council's modern departmental records. It is one of the oldest archive offices in the country and houses many thousands of irreplaceable records depicting all aspects of Bristol's life from the twelfth century onwards. Many fascinating and significant moments are recorded, such as the granting of county status to the town in 1373 (the first English borough to be given this distinction) and its elevation to the status of a city in 1542. Visitors from all over the world come to the city every year simply to carry out research in the Record Office.

TOP LEFT: THE COUNCIL CHAMBER. LEFT: STATUE OF AN ELIZABETHAN SEAMAN. TOP CENTRE: SPLENDID CLOCK WITH WIND INDICATOR. BOTTOM CENTRE: LATE FIFTEENTH-CENTURY MAYOR-MAKING CEREMONY AS SHOWN IN RICART'S CALENDAR. RIGHT: DETAIL OF THE STATE SWORD OF 1752.

BRISTOL CATHEDRAL

The history of Bristol's cathedral dates back to the twelfth century, when Robert Fitzhardinge, Provost of Bristol and ancestor of the Earls of Berkeley, founded an Augustinian abbey overlooking the river on the supposed site of St. Augustine's meeting with the Celtic Christians in the seventh century.

Like many of the country's great churches, it took many centuries to assume its current form. It would have been a church of reasonably modest scale, although of some importance, when it was first built in about 1140.

Already by the second half of that century it was being enlarged and acquired the splendid Norman Chapter House which, with the lower half of the great gateway, still stands. This chapter house is regarded as England's finest example of Romanesque building of its kind, and although the east end of the room had to be reconstructed after being damaged during riots in 1831, it is largely in its original state. The design and detail of the masonry are quite spectacular, and a beautiful example of the skill of some early church masons.

In about 1220 the chapel now known as the Elder Lady Chapel was built. The carving in the chapel is very

TOP: THE NORTHERN ASPECT OF THE CATHEDRAL FROM COLLEGE GREEN. BOTTOM: DETAIL FROM THE TOMB OF ABBOT NEWBERRY.

fine, portraying some splendidly eccentric animals derived from the bestiaries of the time, including a monkey playing the bagpipes accompanied by a ram on the violin.

About 150 years after its inception the abbey gained its real master builder, Edmund Knowle, abbot from 1306 to 1332. In 1298 he started work on a new eastern choir limb and lady chapel for the abbey, following a practice popular at the time of building out eastward from the church to create more space and separate the choir from the congregation. The style in which Abbot Knowle built this eastern end of the church was of such a pioneering design that it became the first of the great 'hall churches' of Europe, with its high side aisles and tall aisle windows filling the building with light. It still remains unique in this country.

By 1330 the choir and east end of the Abbey were finished. The east window in the Eastern Lady Chapel contains some of England's finest medieval heraldic glass, and around its walls are beautiful stellate niches which now hold the effigies of a number of fifteenth-century abbots. On the altar is a pair of magnificent

TOP DETAIL: ONE OF THE MANY FINE MISERICORDS, THIS
CARVING DEPICTS A SCENE FROM THE STORY OF *REYNARD THE
FOX*. ABOVE LEFT: SAXON CARVING. LEFT: TOMB OF BISHOP BUSH.
MAIN PICTURE: THE NORMAN CHAPTER HOUSE.

candlesticks given to the cathedral in 1712 as a thanksgiving donation by the privateers who rescued Alexander Selkirk—the castaway immortalised by Daniel Defoe as Robinson Crusoe.

Fifteenth-century additions to the abbey were the massive central tower and transept roofs, built to replace the flat Norman wooden roofs of the original church. The tower contains its original bell-frame and three bells—the others were confiscated by Edward VI and presumably melted down.

In 1539 the abbey was dissolved by Henry VIII, and in 1542 was reconstituted as the Cathedral Church of the newly created Diocese of Bristol. At the time of the dissolution, the nave was in the process of being rebuilt. The rebuilding was abandoned, and the nave walled off at the western Tower Arch, to be rebuilt to extraordinary effect nearly 300 years later.

Eminent Victorian church architect George Edmund Street's ambitious plan to complete the work begun by Abbot Knowle was accepted in 1867, and work began in 1868. He built the new nave on the line of the fourteenth-century foundations he had discovered, and his instructions were 'to build such another nave as Knowle would have created had he lived.' The results can be regarded as a truly great achievement of the Victorian Gothic imagination, and an extraordinarily executed mark of respect to a medieval master builder. The western end of the nave, with its two fine towers, was finished after Street's death under the supervision of J. L. Pearson.

Among the many fascinating architectural and historical details in the cathedral are a number of interesting monuments. One of them, the rather grim tomb of Bishop Bush, Bristol's first Bishop, who died in 1558, stands out as the first dateable piece of Renaissance detail in the city. In the Berkeley Chapel, beyond the South Choir Aisle, is buried Joan, wife of Thomas Lord Berkeley, who died in 1309. Also here is the only medieval candelabrum in England, which was for many years kept in the Temple Church in Bristol

LEFT: MONUMENT TO SIR JOHN AND LADY YOUNG WITH A DETAIL SHOWN ABOVE. RIGHT: EASTERN LADY CHAPEL. TOP RIGHT: THE MEDIEVAL CANDELABRUM.

before being given to the cathedral for safekeeping during the Second World War. The fine organ was built in 1685 by the best English builder of the time, Renatus Harris; all the pipework and many of the stops are original.

In 1962, the South Choir Aisle window, by Keith New, was installed to replace glass damaged during the Second World War. In 1980 a sculpture by Naomi Blake, called *Refugee*, was erected on the West Lawn. It is dedicated to all victims of racial persecution, and provides a fitting contemporary addition to a building whose history spans nine centuries.

THE ABBEY GATEWAY

Facing out to College Green is the gatehouse to the Norman Abbey built on the site in the twelfth century, most of whose surviving buildings are now incorporated into the Cathedral School. The splendid archway to the gate is clearly the work of a talented master mason, contemporary with the original monastery, while the upper portion was built by Abbot Elyot in the early sixteenth century and much reconstructed at the end of the nineteenth.

CENTRAL LIBRARY

Next to the gatehouse, and remarkably in keeping with it, is the Central Library, opened in 1906. It is one of the most widely admired early works of architect Charles Holden. His achievement was to create a perfect neighbour to the gatehouse, with its strong Norman features, whilst avoiding either pastiche or jarring contrast. The resulting juxtaposition of medieval and early modernist styles is one of the most successful architectural marriages in the city.

LEFT: THE WEST FRONT OF THE CATHEDRAL. RIGHT: THE
NORMAN ABBEY GATEWAY.

THE LORD MAYOR'S CHAPEL

Bristol is the only city in the country to have a civic church. Dating back to about 1220 and granted to the city corporation in 1541 after the Dissolution of the Monasteries, it has been the official place of worship for the Lord Mayor since 1722. A seat and magnificent sword-rest in the nave mark the Lord Mayor's place in the congregation even now.

The chapel is the only building remaining above ground of the Hospital of the Gaunts, founded by Maurice de Gaunt in the thirteenth century and later endowed by Henry de Gaunt and Robert de Gourney. The hospital was a religious community for three centuries until its dissolution, when it became closely associated with education in the city.

The chapel has many fine medieval architectural details, and is of interest as a rare surviving example of a church attached to this kind of smaller religious community. It is also remarkable for the French and Flemish stained glass in a number of windows, and for the sixteenth-century Spanish enamel tiles on the floor of the beautiful Poyntz Chapel. There are two striking effigies of the hospital's founders, Maurice de Gaunt and Robert de Gourney, in the South Chapel.

TOP: THE LORD MAYOR'S CHAPEL. BELOW: BRUNEL HOUSE.

BRUNEL HOUSE

It was Brunel's idea that the terminus of the Great Western Railway should be near the heart of the city and the docks. The first part of this scheme was the building of the Royal Western Hotel, designed by prominent architect Richard Shackleton Pope in collaboration with Brunel in 1837. The hotel was planned as a staging post in Brunel's grand design—the linking of London and New York by train and steamship.

It was built on a grand scale in the neoclassical style, blending Ionic columns at ground level with Corinthian half-columns and pilasters on its upper storeys.

Unfortunately, for all its grandeur, the Royal Western Hotel was never a success—perhaps because Bristol docks proved unsuitable for regular steamship services to America. It closed in 1855 and was converted first to Turkish baths, later to a hotel again, and finally to offices. The recent restoration of its splendid façade, with new offices behind, now occupied by Bristol City Council, has brought back its former grandeur.

HARVEYS WINE MUSEUM

⌐ucked away in Denmark Street behind the city centre a unique museum marking Bristol's long association ⌐ith the wine trade. Harveys Wine Museum, devoted ● the art of wine making, is owned and run by one of ⌐e city's best-known companies, the sherry shipper and ⌐ine merchant, John Harvey and Sons. The museum located in the company's underground cellars which ⌐te back to the thirteenth century when they were part ⌐ the Gaunts' Hospital.

PART OF HARVEYS SPLENDID COLLECTION OF GLASS.

The Harvey family became involved in the wine trade at the end of the eighteenth century when the first John Harvey was apprenticed into his uncle's wine firm at the age of 16. The company traded from the same site in Denmark Street from 1796 until 1960, when their expanding business demanded a move to larger, modern premises on part of Bristol's former civic airfield at Whitchurch.

In their vacated city centre cellars, the company decided to create a wine museum, which has been open to the public, by appointment only, since 1965. It houses fine collections of antique items such as corkscrews, bottles, bin labels, decanter labels or bottle tickets, tastevins, coasters, decanters and one of the finest private collections of eighteenth-century English drinking glass. Visitors are allocated one of Harveys' professional guides, who will initiate them into such matters as the functioning of a champagne tap, the definition of a fuddling cup and a butler's friend, whether grapes are really pressed by foot and what an Elizabethan tavern was like. The visit ends with a tasting of six samples of port, sherry or wine, with an expert on hand to guide and explain. The restaurant within the same premises is one of Bristol's finest, and Harveys still maintain a wine shop there.

THE UNICORN FEATURES IN HARVEYS MUSEUM AS A RE-CREATION OF AN ELIZABETHAN TAVERN.

⌐T THE END OF DENMARK AVENUE IS THE TIMBER-FRAME ⌐TCHET INN DATED 1606—A LONE SURVIVOR OF THE AREA DEMOLISHED IN THE 1960s.

TOWERING ABOVE THE HATCHET, THE VAST MECCA LEISURE ENTERTAINMENT CENTRE HAS CINEMAS, SNOOKER CENTRE, SOCIAL CLUB AND A POPULAR SKATING RINK.

THE EYE GALLERY NEARBY SHOWS A LIVELY RANGE OF WORKS BY MAINLY LOCAL PAINTERS AND SCULPTORS.

University and
Brandon Hill

For sheer character, this part of the city is hard to beat. Historic buildings, museums, shops, restaurants and serene open space co-exist within a stone's throw of the splendid Wills' Tower. The rich diversity of people who work or visit here—from students representing many cultures to shoppers to business people—gives the area a special quality that makes a stroll up Park Street or along Queen's Road doubly rewarding.

ST. MICHAEL'S HILL

The ends of the seventeenth and eighteenth centuries were marked by rapid growth beyond the medieval boundaries of the city. St. Michael's Hill, reached from the old town by a walk up Christmas Steps, is still a perfect example of this expansion, thanks to enlightened conservation and restoration.

From St. Michael's Church and Rectory at the foot of the hill, the houses rise in an attractive mixture of architectural styles. Colston's Almshouses were built in 1691 by city benefactor Edward Colston, whilst more modern institutions on the Hill are the Maternity Hospital and the famous Children's Hospital.

THE RED LODGE

The Red Lodge in Park Row contains the only surviving sixteenth-century domestic interior in Bristol. The first-floor suite of oak rooms, culminating in the Great Oak Room with its oak panelling, plasterwork ceiling and carved stone chimneypiece, has changed little since the house was built in about 1590. Early in the eighteenth century, the house was 'modernised', and the Print Room and Reception Room are furnished with gilt and walnut furniture, in vivid contrast to the dark oak of the earlier rooms.

In the nineteenth century the Red Lodge became famous as the first girls' reform school in Britain. It was founded by Mary Carpenter in 1854 and lasted for some 65 years. In 1919 the house was presented to the City of Bristol and has served as a period house museum since the early 1920s. Admission is free.

TOP LEFT: ST. MICHAEL'S HILL. TOP RIGHT: COLSTON'S ALMSHOUSES. BOTTOM: THE LAST SURVIVING SUITE OF SIXTEENTH-CENTURY ROOMS IN BRISTOL CAN BE SEEN IN THE RED LODGE.

UNIVERSITY AND WILLS TOWER

Nineteenth-century Bristol was an affluent urban industrial centre, and many of its prominent citizens felt it needed the prestige of its own university. Two men, the Reverend John Percival, headmaster of the recently founded Clifton College boys' school, and Benjamin Jowett, Master of Balliol College, Oxford, promoted the idea among the city's wealthy patrons and in 1876 the University College of Bristol opened its doors to its first students. The new college was modestly housed in two properties in Park Row, and in keeping with its founders' forward-looking ideas was the first higher educational institution in England to admit women on an equal basis with men.

In 1879 Bristol architect Charles Hanson was commissioned to start work on an impressive college quadrangle. Financial difficulties faced the infant university from the beginning, caused partly by the fact that many of the city's wealthy families were for some time wary of the Nonconformist leanings of its founders. Gradually, with an increase in government funds, the college grew. The Engineering block was added to the quadrangle in 1893, and the Medical School was built and incorporated in the same year. By the turn of the century, the college had the nucleus of all the departments that characterise it today; but it was not until after a long campaign by academic supporters and the offer of £100,000 from Henry Wills, the tobacco millionaire, that full university status was conferred by Royal Charter in 1909.

The Wills family proved to be the university's greatest benefactors. Henry Wills was the first chancellor of the new university and on his death his two sons decided to give the university a new main building in his memory. The Wills Memorial Tower at the top of Park Street was the first of many gifts from the family, and certainly the most prominent.

215 ft. tall, with an Entrance Hall and Great Hall on a massive scale, the Wills Tower has been called the last great Gothic building in England. It was designed by George Oatley, who had already built the Chemistry and Physiology buildings in the quadrangle, and was officially opened by King George V and Queen Mary in 1925.

Over the course of this century, the university has expanded into many parts of the city and gained many new and impressive buildings, but this extraordinary Gothic memorial, dominating the city skyline, remains a unique and much-loved symbol of the academic life of Bristol.

TOP: THE WILLS MEMORIAL BUILDING. RIGHT: SIR GEORGE OATLEY'S DESIGN FOR THE BUILDING DATED 1914. BOTTOM: THE MAGNIFICENT ENTRANCE HALL.

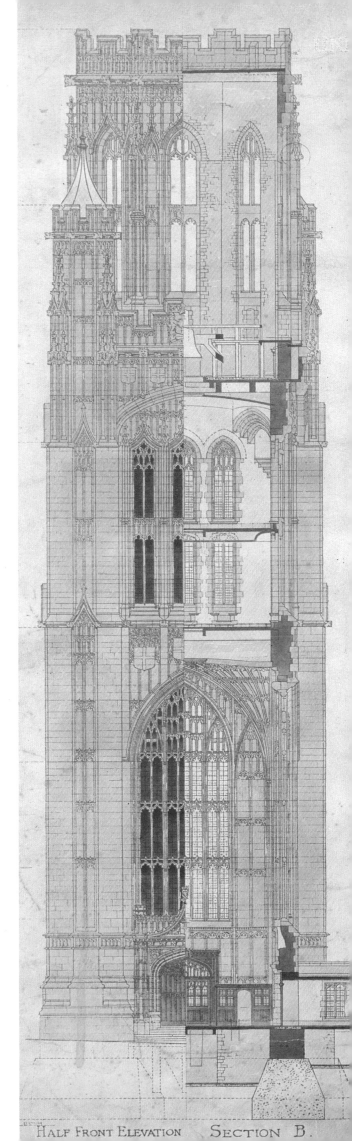

HALF FRONT ELEVATION   SECTION B

CITY MUSEUM AND ART GALLERY

The principal collections of the City Museum and Art Gallery are housed in a fine building in Queen's Road, given by Sir William Wills in 1905, and in a rear extension funded by his cousin, Sir George Wills, and opened in 1930. The museum boasts excellent collections in six main areas—fine art, applied art, Oriental art, world archaeology, geology and natural history—and houses many treasures of national and international significance.

The arts occupy the top floors and the ground floor of the rear hall. Old masters fill one gallery, and include a Bellini showing Christ descending into limbo and a fascinating altarpiece containing the earliest true portrait of a Bristol merchant, Paul Withypool, painted by the Venetian Da Solario in 1514. There are a number of important French paintings and sculptures, including work by Delacroix, Renoir and Seurat. The flourishing nineteenth-century Bristol school features strongly, as might be expected, and other leading British artists from the seventeenth century onwards are well-represented.

In the applied art galleries there is a fine collection of early silver, some of which bears the rare Bristol assay mark, as well as an excellent collection of ceramics in a new gallery devoted to Bristol's historic connections with the pottery trade.

The museum's Oriental art collection is renowned worldwide, and boasts examples of Chinese glass unrivalled outside China. The Oriental galleries also contain superb Chinese pottery from pre-Ming dynasties, and impressive collections of later Chinese and Japanese porcelain, lacquer and bronzes, prints and textiles.

Bristol was for many years a major glassmaking centre, and this local tradition is reflected in the museum's displays, whilst glass from further afield includes the Lazarus Collection of eighteenth-century drinking glasses. The artistry of early glassmakers can be seen in the Bomford Collection from the East Mediterranean, some of which dates back 4,000 years.

TOP DETAIL: PERUVIAN FLASK. TOP: A WORKING REPLICA OF THE BRISTOL BOX KITE OF 1910 HANGS ABOVE THE ENTRANCE HALL. BOTTOM: SUPERB FOSSIL DISPLAYS. RIGHT: AN EARTHENWARE TOMB FIGURE FROM THE CHINESE COLLECTION.

The archaeological history of the South West of England is illustrated in displays of early tools and crafts from the region, dating back to prehistoric times. The fund of local historical artefacts dating from medieval Bristol has been greatly enlarged by post-war rescue archaeology, which has retrieved wonderful examples of local pottery such as the Ham Green ware found in since-vanished Peter Street and now on display.

The Ancient Egyptian collections occupy a comparatively new gallery which explores the themes of death and burial along the Nile. The outstanding art of the early Egyptians can be appreciated in all its splendour in this fine collection; equally as splendid, from neighbouring Assyria, are the three marble reliefs made in the eighth century B.C., and which now dominate the front hall.

Natural history is represented both on a regional and a national level, with displays illustrating the flora and fauna of the area, and excellent study collections to back up the public ones. Many of the exhibits are displayed in models of their natural habitat, whilst fish and other living creatures are housed in aquaria, creating an impression far removed from the static museum model of earlier times. The Natural History Department carries out much valuable fieldwork, and is particularly known for its acclaimed butterfly and dragonfly surveys.

Earliest history is represented by the museum's magnificent geology collections. Despite serious wartime damage, these displays of fossils and minerals are of exceptional quality, and include such recent additions as a huge skull of a pliosaur from Westbury in Wiltshire and an almost intact ichthyosaur which at 35 ft. is one of the largest of its class ever recorded. These examples of the 'sea dragons' of 200 million years ago have proved to be an endless source of fascination for casual visitors and specialists alike.

Educational work is a vital part of the museum's activity in all these areas, and regular programmes of lectures and study sessions are organised to explore and expand the public displays.

TOP LEFT: CHILDREN FROM ST. BARNABAS' SCHOOL LEARN THE TECHNIQUES OF TIE-AND-DYE AS PART OF THE MUSEUM'S EDUCATION SERVICE. TOP RIGHT: MODEL SHOWING THE BRISTOL AREA 200 MILLION YEARS AGO. MAIN PICTURE: ICHTHYOSAURUS. DETAIL RIGHT: REDCLIFFE WARE WINE JUG. BOTTOM LEFT: 4,000-YEAR-OLD CHINESE EARTHENWARE VASE. BOTTOM RIGHT: RE-CREATION OF AN EGYPTIAN TOMB.

PARK STREET AND QUEEN'S ROAD

Park Street and Queen's Road link the centre of Bristol to Clifton and Redland, and have been two of the city's principal thoroughfares since the growth of Bristol in the eighteenth century. Although both suffered extensive damage during the Second World War, rebuilding has been quite carefully carried out to blend in with what survives of the Georgian grandeur of the surrounding town houses.

In the 1760s Park Street began the residential move uphill which eventually transformed Clifton into a suburb of Bristol from the independent spa resort it had been. Much of Park Street was laid out by the gifted architectural family of Thomas and William Paty, and the elegance of their design can best be seen in some of the roads off Park Street: Great George Street, Charlotte Street and Berkeley Square.

Top: PARK STREET, ILLUMINATED FOR CHRISTMAS, BOASTS A VARIETY OF CLOTHES AND SPECIALITY SHOPS PLUS WINE BARS AND RESTAURANTS.

ROYAL WEST OF ENGLAND ACADEMY

The Royal West of England Academy began life in 1844 when a group of Bristol art patrons and artists met to discuss the establishment of an academy for the teaching and exhibition of art and sculpture.

It was not until about ten years later that enough money was raised to build a permanent home for the Academy. The building, with a suitably Renaissance-style façade and Grecian-inspired galleries inside, was inaugurated in 1858.

In 1913 a new frontage was built to enlarge the galleries, and in the same year the academy was granted a Royal Charter by King George V.

The R.W.A. has always been, and continues to be, an independent organisation administered by its council and funded through its own work. It presents a wide range of exhibitions by members and non-members, and continues its long-standing connection with architecture in the city by awarding an architectural scholarship every year.

TOP: THE SPLENDID R.W.A. BUILDING. BELOW: THE ANNUAL OPEN
EXHIBITION IS A MAJOR EVENT IN THE REGIONAL ART CALENDAR.

43

VICTORIA ROOMS

The Victoria Rooms were built for public meetings and other gatherings by a consortium of local businessmen at the very beginning of Queen Victoria's reign. They were designed by local architect Charles Dyer, with a pediment sculpture by local sculptor Jabez Tyley, and

opened in 1844. In front of this imposing portico the forecourt and splendid neo-baroque fountains were laid out at the beginning of this century as a memorial to King Edward VII, whose statue stands there.

In 1920 the building was bought by Sir John Wills as a students' union for the university. Since the building of a new, purpose-built union, the Victoria Rooms have been used for concerts, lectures and performances.

BERKELEY SQUARE

Berkeley Square is one of the tranquil, oddly secluded parts of central Bristol which immediately bring to mind the Georgian city of 200 years ago. Designed by Thomas Paty and his son William, the square was begun in 1787 when the city was expanding onto the hills around it and the wealth of Bristol merchants was being channelled into residential architecture of great elegance.

The poet John Addington Symonds was born at No. 7 in 1840 and John Loudon Macadam, the inventor of tar 'macadam' for roads, lived in the square when he was general surveyor of the Bristol District Turnpike Trust from 1815 to 1825.

In the south-east corner of the gardens is a replica of the upper section of the medieval High Cross of Bristol, the original of which stands in the gardens at Stourhead in Wiltshire.

LEFT: THE VICTORIA ROOMS. TOP RIGHT: DETAIL FROM THE REPLICA OF BRISTOL HIGH CROSS NOW IN BERKELEY SQUARE. BOTTOM: BERKELEY SQUARE.

BRANDON HILL

The distinctively shaped Brandon Hill, crowned by the Cabot Tower, lays claim to being the oldest park in Bristol, and provides one of the most accessible and pleasant open-spaces in the whole of the modern city. As a quaint hangover from much earlier times, the townspeople of Bristol still have the right to dry their washing on the hedges and bushes and, within specific hours, to beat their carpets on the hill.

During the Civil War sieges of 1643–5, defences were erected here for some of the city's heaviest fighting and there are still some traces of the earthworks to be seen.

The hill boasts a fine collection of ornamental trees, an imposing rockery and a delightful mixture of woodland, scrub-heath and meadow which attracts a wide range of wildlife. It recently became the first urban park in the country to include a nature park.

CABOT TOWER

One of Bristol's best-known central landmarks is the Cabot Tower, which stands on Brandon Hill and commands a magnificent view over the city and towards the Mendip Hills. The foundation stone was laid in 1897 by the Marquis of Dufferin in a ceremony of great pomp to commemorate the fourth centenary of John Cabot's voyage of discovery from Bristol to mainland America. The tower was officially opened by the Marquis, with equal ceremony, the following year. A commemorative tower was erected almost simultaneously in Canada on Signal Hill, at the entrance to St. John's Harbour, Newfoundland. Built in red sandstone with Bath stone dressings, Cabot Tower was designed in the late Tudor Gothic style in use at the time when North America was discovered. It is 105 ft. high and is topped with a figure representing Commerce standing on a globe.

TOP: BRANDON HILL AND THE CABOT TOWER. BOTTOM: THE CLIMB TO THE TOP OF THE TOWER IS REWARDED WITH PANORAMIC VIEWS.

ST. GEORGE'S CHURCH

St. George's, Brandon Hill, is central Bristol's only 'Waterloo Church', built by the Church Commissioners with parliamentary money in the general expansion of cities after the Battle of Waterloo in 1815. It was built in 1823 in the classical style by Robert Smirke, who had designed the new Opera House at Covent Garden in London.

The church was declared redundant in 1984, and leased for 50 years to St. George's Music Trust at a peppercorn rent. Its beautifully proportioned interior has a perfect acoustic for music, and provides excellent performing facilities. Radio 3 lunchtime concerts are regularly broadcast from the church, and the building is now one of the best-known concert venues in the region.

THE GEORGIAN HOUSE

The Georgian House, situated in Great George Street, was built by the local architect William Paty for John Pretor Pinney, a wealthy sugar merchant. Three of the six floors are open to visitors and have been furnished to show how the house might have looked when Pinney and his family moved in in 1791. Admission is free.

On the ground floor, John Pinney's Study contains the only original furniture in the house: a bureau-bookcase and two built-in bookcases. The Breakfast Parlour and Eating Room now open into each other but could once be divided by folding doors. In the Eating Room is displayed part of Pinney's Chinese porcelain dinner service decorated with his coat-of-arms.

The main Drawing Room was on the first floor, well away from the noise and dirt of the street. From the windows John Pinney would have had a good view of his ships leaving and entering the harbour. In the Library is a superb collector's cabinet fitted with small drawers which might have housed a collection of insects or coins. The small adjoining room is now furnished as a bedroom.

In the basement are the domestic offices: Kitchen, Laundry, Pantry and Housekeeper's Room. The Kitchen retains its open range and bread-oven for cooking. The copper and brass cooking pans are displayed on the built-in dresser, while smaller gadgets can be seen in the Larder. The Second Kitchen also served as the Laundry. Water was pumped up from the tank below and heated in two copper boilers. The rocker-washer and box-mangle are the forerunners of today's labour-saving laundry equipment. At the front of the house, with a good view of the front door, is the Housekeeper's Room. A most unusual feature is the cold-water plunge bath which John Pinney used as a spartan substitute for the morning swim he enjoyed every day during his years in the West Indies.

TOP LEFT: ST. GEORGE'S CHURCH. TOP RIGHT: A LIVE BROADCAST OF THE GUILDHALL STRING ENSEMBLE IN PROGRESS. BOTTOM: THE GEORGIAN HOUSE.

47

Redcliffe and
Temple Meads

Visitors' first impressions of this corner of Bristol may be dominated by thundering traffic and the hubbub of city life. But in fact the area is full of surprises. Places of interest include the world's oldest surviving major railway terminus and, according to Queen Elizabeth I, the finest parish church in England.

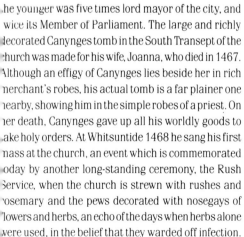

...he younger was five times lord mayor of the city, and twice its Member of Parliament. The large and richly decorated Canynges tomb in the South Transept of the church was made for his wife, Joanna, who died in 1467. Although an effigy of Canynges lies beside her in rich merchant's robes, his actual tomb is a far plainer one nearby, showing him in the simple robes of a priest. On her death, Canynges gave up all his worldly goods to take holy orders. At Whitsuntide 1468 he sang his first mass at the church, an event which is commemorated today by another long-standing ceremony, the Rush Service, when the church is strewn with rushes and rosemary and the pews decorated with nosegays of flowers and herbs, an echo of the days when herbs alone were used, in the belief that they warded off infection.

Over the years alterations and additions to the church reflected the concerns and styles of the changing times. The Victorians undertook major repair and embellishment, installed new pews and stained glass and constructed the present spire in 1872.

Memorials in the church bear witness to famous Bristolians and to associations the city has held with notable figures over the centuries. On the north wall of the nave are the arms and armour of Admiral Sir William Penn, commander-in-chief of the fleet during the war with the Dutch in the 1650s, whose son William founded the American state of Pennsylvania. The famous 'Handel Window' in the North Choir Aisle, illustrating scenes from *The Messiah*, was installed in 1859 to commemorate the centenary of the death of the composer, who frequently visited the church and composed on its organ.

The Chapel of St. John the Baptist is now called the American Chapel, having been restored by friends of St. Mary Redcliffe in the United States. Above the entrance is a whale-bone, thought to have been brought back to Bristol in 1497 by John Cabot from his voyage to Newfoundland. Most of the remaining medieval glass in the church has been collected into the two windows in this chapel.

There is also a wooden figure of Queen Elizabeth I—most probably the figurehead of a ship. Elizabeth played a significant role in the history of the church, apart from her much-quoted affection for it, in that she returned to it some of the endowments seized by Edward VI and later her father, Henry VIII, thus restoring much of its wealth. She also agreed to the foundation of a 'Free Grammar and Writing School' in a nearby chapel in 1571. It was transferred to the Lady Chapel of the church in 1762, thus establishing the long association between the church and education which survives today.

One final fascinating feature of the church is the muniment room above the North Porch, where the young Bristol poet Thomas Chatterton claimed to have discovered the medieval manuscripts that made him briefly famous. When they were exposed as fakes, Chatterton committed suicide; a memorial stone to him can be seen in the South Transept and another, to his family, in the churchyard.

TOP: THE TWO TOMBS OF CANYNGES; HE IS ACTUALLY BURIED IN THE LATER TOMB, SHOWN ON THE LEFT. MAIN PICTURE: THE SUPERB HEXAGONAL OUTER PORCH. BOTTOM LEFT: THE RIB OF A COW-WHALE REPUTEDLY PRESENTED TO THE CITY BY JOHN CABOT. BOTTOM RIGHT: THE ARMS AND ARMOUR OF ADMIRAL SIR WILLIAM PENN.

ABOVE: THIS PAINTING FROM THE TATE GALLERY DRAMATISES
THE SUICIDE OF THE POET CHATTERTON. RIGHT: CHATTERTON
HOUSE. BELOW: THE PHOENIX GLASS KILN IN THE 1880s.

CHATTERTON HOUSE

Chatterton House contains no exhibits at present, but is of considerable interest since it was the birthplace of the poet Thomas Chatterton (1752–1770), son of the local schoolteacher whose house this was and who died three months before Thomas's birth.

The house is architecturally important, being a rare survivor in Bristol of the class of smaller early eighteenth-century dwelling; and unique for the attachment to it, in the twentieth century, of the façade of the original schoolhouse, which was demolished when Redcliffe Way was built. This historic building is cared for by the City Museum and Art Gallery and can be viewed on application to the Assistant Director of Arts on giving reasonable notice.

THE GLASS KILN

One of Bristol's largest hotels contains a curious memento of what was once a thriving industry in the city. The Kiln Restaurant in the Hilton International complex in Redcliffe Way marks the site of the Phoenix Glass Kiln, the last and one of the most successful glasshouses in Bristol.

The eighteenth century saw the rise of Bristol as a major glass-making centre, with as many as sixteen glasshouses operating in the city. The Phoenix, named after the inn on whose site it was built, was the last to open, and produced what was known as flint glass. When it opened in 1785 the industry was already in decline in Bristol, due largely to the economic effects of the wars with France and America and the rise of manufacturing centres in the North of England. However, the company weathered the crisis and continued in business long after most other glasshouses had been forced to close.

Glass production finally stopped in Bristol in 1920, but the 65 ft. kiln was a landmark in the city until the 1930s, when most of it was demolished. The base is now incorporated in a much-reduced form into the hotel restaurant.

ABOVE: THE VICTORIAN SPLENDOUR OF BRUNEL'S BRISTOL OLD STATION. RIGHT: THE RESTORED BOARDROOM. BELOW: THE INTERIOR DURING THE STATION'S HEYDAY.

BRISTOL OLD STATION

Alongside the present mainline station at Temple Meads, the original Terminus of the Great Western Railway survives as the undoubted masterpiece of railway building, the first example of a great piece of architecture created for a railway company.

The first proposal for a railway between London and Bristol was made in 1824, but it was not until 1833 that a board of directors was formed for the company named the Great Western Railway, and two years later that a bill to construct the line was authorised by Parliament. The young engineer Isambard Kingdom Brunel, who had already started work on the Clifton Suspension Bridge, was appointed chief engineer for the project.

In 1840 the Great Western line and Terminus were completed, at a total cost of over six and a half million pounds. The Great Train Shed was over 220 ft. long (80 ft. longer than Bristol Cathedral) and its 72 ft. single roof span was the wonder of the age. Behind majestic stone façades were all the functions of a major railway interchange: passenger facilities, engine shed, water tower, boardroom, offices, living accommodation, stables and warehouses.

Brunel's great Terminus was superseded before long by the building of the new Temple Meads station at right angles to it in the 1870s. It became a neglected backwater of the station, occasionally threatened with demolition, until rescued from obscurity by the Brunel Engineering Centre Trust in 1980. The Trust took on a 99-year full-repairing lease at a peppercorn rent from British Rail to restore and convert the building, with the help of sponsoring companies and employment schemes. The Great Train Shed can now be seen in some of its former glory, with restoration work still in progress. In the course of renovation it has been used for exhibitions, functions and sports events, and now houses the Exploratory, the hands-on science centre.

THE EXPLORATORY

The Exploratory 'hands-on' science centre, housed in Brunel's Old Station at Temple Meads from June 1989, is an appropriate link between nineteenth-century scientific innovation and twentieth-century education.

The Exploratory opened in temporary accommodation in February 1987 and won the AA's 'Best Museum of the Future' award for 1988. Inspired by the success of American museums like the San Francisco Exploratorium, its aim is to encourage people, particularly young people, to learn about science and basic scientific principles through participation and enjoyment rather than through static museum displays.

All the exhibits or 'plores'—experiments for exploring—can be handled and activated, making science fun and accessible, and bringing to life the fascination and relevance of phenomena like magnetism and the refraction of light, the perception of colour, or some of the principles governing momentum and gravity. Visitors can build wooden arches to investigate the effects of stress, try out a momentum platform or a gyroscope chair, interact with the glowing gases of a plasma globe, or see a Van de Graaff generator and a wave machine in action. Explanations are printed alongside each 'plore', and 'pilots' are on hand to offer further help and explanation wherever necessary.

TEMPLE MEADS

Bristol's railway station is architecturally unique, and is the largest group of grade 1 listed railway buildings in the country. The main passenger station in use now was built in the 1870s, when Bristol Old Station, built by Brunel in 1840, became too small for the three railway companies serving Bristol. The expansion of Temple Meads was undertaken by Sir Matthew Digby Wyatt, who had worked with Brunel on Paddington station and who built a splendid Gothic edifice much in keeping with his friend's ambitions for the Bristol Terminus. Further expansion in the 1930s created the station as it exists today, a fascinating blend of railway architecture providing a modern, high-speed service on the route originally masterminded by the nineteenth century's greatest engineer.

Top: SCIENCE BROUGHT TO LIFE IN DRAMATIC FASHION AT THE EXPLORATORY. BOTTOM: THE VICTORIAN FAÇADE OF TEMPLE MEADS STATION.

THE WOOLHALL

The Woolhall in St. Thomas Street was built in 1830 as Bristol's wool exchange. It fell almost immediately into disuse, served as a billet for the dragoons brought down from London to quell the Bristol riots in 1831, and was then used for the next 150 years as a general warehouse.

It has recently been restored and converted, with offices on the upper floors, and a pub—the Fleece and Firkin—on the ground floor. It is the only pub in Bristol to brew its own beer.

TEMPLE CHURCH

Largely destroyed by wartime bombing and now preserved by the Department of the Environment, the Temple (Holy Cross) Church is characterised primarily by its distinctive leaning tower. The church was founded in about 1145 by the Order of the Knights Templar. The tower was added at the end of the fourteenth century. Built like the famous campanile at Pisa on soft soil, the tower soon began to lean westwards. The top of the tower was added a little later and consequently leans at a slightly different angle.

VICTORIA STREET

Victoria Street was laid out in the 1860s, during the extensive Victorian rebuilding of Redcliffe, to create an approach to the city from the new railway station at Temple Meads. Many of the offices and warehouses that lined the street have disappeared, but it is still possible to imagine its Victorian appearance from the few remaining buildings of the time, with their typical arcaded brick façades. One long-standing landmark in the street is Ye Shakespeare Inn, one of the oldest pubs in Bristol, which dates from 1636.

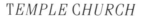

MAIN PICTURE: THE LEANING TOWER OF TEMPLE CHURCH. TOP RIGHT: THE FLEECE AND FIRKIN, QUIET AT LUNCHTIMES, BECOMES A POPULAR ROCK AND JAZZ VENUE MOST EVENINGS. RIGHT: THE SHAKESPEARE INN. VICTORIA STREET.

REDCLIFFE CAVES

Beneath the high ground of Redcliffe lies an extraordinary network of caves and tunnels whose history is, like many such places, made up of fact and legend in equal measure.

The entrance to the caves is from Phoenix Wharf, and was probably built when the caves were 'discovered' in 1768. Before this, a series of openings in the cliff-face had long been known to lead into a network of tunnels under the hill. There are many tales of their occupants and uses over the years, dating back to King Alfred, who was believed to have taken refuge from the Danes there. Monks from St. John's Hospital in the Middle Ages were said to have carved out meditation cells deep in the caves, and passages are believed to lead off the crypt in St. Mary Redcliffe Church. Stories are also told of French and Spanish prisoners being put to work in the caverns.

In the eighteenth century the caves were used as warehouses by the glasshouses which flourished at the time around the docks. Sandstone from the caves may have been used in the manufacturing of glass, served as ships' ballast, was sprinkled on the floor of taverns and was even used to fill pot-holes in the roads.

Having long existed as a little-known subterranean part of the city, the caves and the wharf itself are currently being considered for their tourist potential, and may well reveal their secrets before long.

ABOVE: BRISTOL AND BATH CRUISERS BASED AT PHOENIX WHARF SERVE THREE-COURSE MEALS AS THEY TOUR THE HARBOUR. TOP LEFT: CITY COUNCIL ENGINEERS CARRY OUT FREQUENT INSPECTIONS INSIDE REDCLIFFE CAVES. BOTTOM: IN RECENT YEARS, THE CENTRE OF BRISTOL HAS EXPERIENCED A BOOM IN COMMERCIAL DEVELOPMENT.

REDCLIFFE PARADE

Bristol in the eighteenth century grew fast, and with this growth came a great expansion of residential building. This was the age of the terrace, and Redcliffe Parade, now carefully restored, gives an idea of the style in which the city was developing.

The older part of the parade was built in about 1770; later building accompanied the completion of the New Cut, which greatly opened up the harbour area. Perched on the top of the sandstone cliff which gives the area its name, the parade has a wonderful view of the harbour. Access to the docks is via a donkey-ramp once used to carry goods up from the warehouses on the wharf.

TOP LEFT: THE VIEW OF THE HARBOUR FROM REDCLIFFE PARADE IN VICTORIAN TIMES. BOTTOM: REDCLIFFE PARADE.

Hotwells

Bristol Historic Harbour, in many ways the focal point of the city's regeneration, contains such a diversity of attractions that three chapters of this book are devoted to it. If only for editorial convenience, the harbour has been divided into the Hotwells, St. Augustine's Reach and King Street/Welsh Back areas.

Hotwells is at the western end of the harbour. Here the lock system protects the city from flood tides and gives access to the sea by way of the tidal River Avon. Timber wharfs have been swept away and replaced by splendid visitor attractions and a thriving resident community. But the sand wharfs and boat building and repairing businesses which flourish there add the authentic note of a working waterway.

NOVA SCOTIA

The Nova Scotia pub is a highly popular social spot, particularly in the summer when the outside seating area on Nova Scotia Place offers an excellent vantage point from which to watch the harbour traffic and enjoy the view across to Hotwells and Clifton. Right in front of the pub is the original Junction Lock, part of the construction of the Floating Harbour in the early nineteenth century. On the quayside opposite the pub are the Dock Cottages, which date from 1831.

Top: THE POPULAR NOVA SCOTIA PUB HAS A SPLENDID OUTLOOK
TO THE DOCK COTTAGES (PICTURED BELOW). TOP RIGHT: THE
PUMPHOUSE—A FORMER HYDRAULIC ENGINE HOUSE, NOW A
POPULAR HARBOURSIDE PUB.

UNDERFALL YARD

This is the site of the dam across the Avon, constructed at the beginning of the nineteenth century as part of the non-tidal 'Floating Harbour' for Bristol. At first, surplus water flowed over the dam, which was consequently known as the Overfall. However, when the new Floating Harbour began to silt up, the young engineer Isambard Kingdom Brunel created a series of culverts beneath the dam to drain and scour the harbour, and the site took on its new name.

The Port of Bristol Authority's Workshops were established there in 1884, and the yard is now a store of fascinating industrial machinery, including most of the original steam-driven machinery. The red-brick hydraulic engine house originally housed two steam-engines to power the gates, capstans and bridges of the Floating Harbour, which were replaced in 1908 by three electric ram-pumps, still working well today. The City Council plans to open these buildings to the public.

Top: ROYAL YORK CRESCENT FORMS A POWERFUL BACKDROP TO NOVA SCOTIA PLACE. BOTTOM: VICTORIAN ENGINEERING EQUIPMENT IS STILL IN USE IN THE UNDERFALL YARD WORKSHOPS.

TOP: THE COTTAGE, NOW A POPULAR HARBOURSIDE PUB WITH BALTIC WHARF LEISURE CENTRE BEHIND. BELOW: THIS SAND WHARF ACROSS THE WATER FROM BALTIC WHARF IS THE FINAL REMAINING INDUSTRY IN THE CITY DOCKS.

BALTIC WHARF

Along with much of Bristol's harbour, Baltic Wharf has changed enormously in the past few years. Formerly a busy timber wharf and the site of commercial warehousing and shipping berths, this area is now the centre of the recreational facilities in the harbour. With the reduction of commercial shipping, and the decline in related dockside industries, maintenance of the harbour no longer required the same staffing or engineering capacity and many of the dockside buildings found other uses connected with the water sports and leisure activities on the increase in the area.

In 1977 the City Council began the development of the wharf by converting the early Victorian Harbour Master's cottage and a large Dutch barn into the Baltic Wharf Leisure Centre. This is now a lively and popular centre for all kinds of water sports, with a dinghy park, sailing club, canoe club, rowing club and waterskiing club. The Cottage Inn, once part of the warehousing on the wharf, is now a popular meeting place in this part of the harbour.

Next to the Leisure Centre, and occupying a site which must be exceptional for a city centre, is a touring caravan park, developed by the City Council in conjunction with the Caravan Club of Great Britain. Originally an experiment in response to demand from holidaymakers in the South West, it has become an extremely popular site which even gets booked up at Christmastime.

Another recent addition to the dockside is the Baltic Wharf housing development, one of a number of residential schemes in the harbour which have contributed to the dramatic regeneration of the area

THIS SUCCESSFUL HOUSING DEVELOPMENT, BETWEEN BALTIC
WHARF AND ALBION DOCKYARD, HAS REVITALISED THIS AREA OF
THE HARBOUR.

ALBION DOCKYARD

From 1920 this yard was the home of Hillhouse Sons & Co., who, in 1813, built Bristol's first two steamship tugs. In 1976 the yard launched the last commercial vessel from Bristol—the *Miranda Guinness*—built by the city's premier ship builders, Charles Hill & Co. Ltd.

It was then bought by the City Council and developed into a thriving marina and boatyard. All sorts of pleasure boats are moored in the 150-berth marina, and the place hums with boat repairs and renovations. A number of related businesses like sailmaking and boatbuilding have been established around the yard.

BRISTOL PACKET

The Bristol Packet offers a narrowboat touring service around the main places of interest in the Historic Harbour. The *Tower Belle* is a traditional river steamer, built in 1920, and the narrowboat 'Redshank' is a canal boat, decorated as she would have been in her cargo-carrying days with the traditional roses and castles. Both boats tour around the docks, visiting the pubs for a special dockside pub tour, and go up-river on longer tours as well as down the Avon Gorge towards the Bristol Channel.

ABOVE: THE BRISTOL PACKET. TOP LEFT: THE CHARLES HILL SHIPYARD BEFORE CLOSURE. TOP RIGHT: THE BOATYARD. MAIN PICTURE: THE TRANSFORMED SHIPYARD, NOW RE-NAMED BRISTOL MARINA.

MARITIME HERITAGE CENTRE

Housed in an elegant new building, opened in July 1985 by Her Majesty the Queen, the Maritime Heritage Centre brings alive the history of Bristol's historic harbour and vividly illustrates 200 years of shipbuilding in the Port. It features a famous collection of models, paintings and relics assembled by Bristol's last large-scale shipbuilders, Charles Hill & Sons, and which now forms part of the City of Bristol Museum and Art Gallery's technology collections.

Bristol was famous in the eighteenth century for producing strong, seaworthy vessels and its port and mercantile trade was then second only to London. Unfortunately, the narrow harbour and hazardous tidal river Avon connecting it with the Bristol Channel eventually restricted the city's shipbuilding industry and brought about its decline. Although no longer the major industry it was, steel shipbuilding continues today in the Bristol Marina. The maintenance and restoration of many leisure and historic craft keep alive the traditional skills of the shipbuilder, in a variety of materials ranging from wood, through iron and steel to modern plastics.

A display in the Maritime Centre showing reconstructions of the gun-deck of an eighteenth-century frigate, a unique iron-hulled steam dredger designed by Brunel and a modern welded-steel hull, illustrate the changes in shipbuilding since 1770. Lifelike figures show shipwrights working with wood, riveting iron and welding steel. The balcony of the centre provides a superb platform to view Bristol's changing historic harbour. The centre is the entrance-point for the S.S. *Great Britain* and is open all through the year with the exceptions of Christmas Day and Boxing Day.

ABOVE: THE MARITIME HERITAGE CENTRE FEATURES SUPERB DISPLAYS ILLUSTRATING SHIPBUILDING IN BRISTOL (LEFT AND BELOW).

S.S. *GREAT BRITAIN*

The S.S. *Great Britain* was built in Bristol and launched on 19 July 1843—the first propeller-driven ocean-going iron ship in history. Now undergoing restoration in the very same dry dock in which she was built, she is one of Bristol's major visitor attractions.

When the ship was launched, both her size and design were revolutionary. At the time, American companies had a virtual monopoly on North Atlantic passenger trade, with their fast sailing packets providing a reliable, regular service between New York and Liverpool. Brunel's *Great Western*, launched six years earlier by the Great Western Steamship Company, had successfully challenged this monopoly, and proved that it was possible for a large, wooden steamship with paddle-wheels to make the crossing without running out of coal. He then planned a bigger, improved sister ship, to be called the *City of New York*.

His plans, however, changed dramatically as a result of two decisions, the first of which was to build his ship of iron. This meant that it would be far too heavy for any existing slipways in Bristol harbour, and so a new dry dock was specially excavated and equipped. The second change of plan occurred when a small experimental vessel, the *Archimedes*, arrived in Bristol with a new screw-propeller system. Brunel then decided that his new ship would also be propeller, not paddle, driven. Her name was changed to the *Great Britain* and building began.

Apart from these major innovations, among other novel details was a huge engine skylight on the deck, which also covered the top of the massive driving wheel—a source of intense fascination to her first passengers.

The launch of the *Great Britain* was an occasion of great celebration throughout the city. Bells and cannon rang out and Prince Albert, the Prince Consort, travelled down from London on Brunel's Great Western Railway. Late the following year, 1844, she was ready for trials in the Bristol Channel, but experienced some difficulty in passing through the narrow locks leading out of the Cumberland Basin. Coping-stones on the locks were hastily removed, and she was finally towed down the Avon by tug on 12 December 1844.

After touring to London and Liverpool to be admired by vast crowds of visitors, the *Great Britain* embarked on her maiden voyage across the Atlantic. The passage to New York took 14 days, and she made

the return crossing in 13½ days at an average of nine knots. On her fifth journey, disaster struck. She ran aground on the beach of Dundrum Bay on the East Coast of Ireland, and had to be towed back to Liverpool for repair. The Great Western Steamship Company was forced to put her up for sale, having failed to insure her adequately. She was bought in December 1850 by Gibbs, Bright and Company of Liverpool, who modified and refitted her for use as a passenger ship to Australia. Over the next 26 years she circumnavigated the globe 32 times between Liverpool and Melbourne, carrying the forebears of a probable quarter of a million present-day Australians.

Once her passenger days were over, she was bought for use as a cargo ship and had all her passenger accommodation removed. Whilst travelling round Cape Horn in May 1886, she got into difficulties in very high winds, lost both fore and main topgallant masts and began to let in water severely. She reached shelter in Port Stanley in the Falkland Islands, and never sailed again. For many years she was used as a store ship, and was then towed out to lie forgotten in Sparrow Cove.

In the 1950s independent initiatives were begun both in America and in Britain to salvage and restore her. Finally, in 1968, the British formed the 'S.S. *Great Britain* Project', and raised the necessary money to send a salvage party to the Falkland Islands with a submersible pontoon and the technical expertise to bring the ship back—a project looked on by many as hopelessly optimistic.

On 12 April the S.S. *Great Britain* was lifted clear of the water and onto the pontoon; she was then floated back to Bristol, arriving at the dry dock by extraordinary coincidence on 19 July, the anniversary of her launch.

The 'S.S. *Great Britain* Project' was given the dry dock as a permanent site by the City Council, and the ship was put on public display. Restoration work is already far advanced, and the S.S. *Great Britain* will ultimately appear as near as possible to the ship that Brunel built 150 years ago.

TOP: THE S.S. *GREAT BRITAIN* AT SEA. BOTTOM: THE RESTORED PROPELLER AND RUDDER. OPPOSITE PAGE: THE SHIP IN THE ORIGINAL DRY-DOCK IN WHICH SHE WAS BUILT.

St. Augustine's Reach

While this central section of the Historic Harbour contains imaginative office and housing developments, much of it is devoted to a truly remarkable spectrum of leisure uses. A range of thriving cultural and recreational facilities, together with shops, pubs and restaurants and a programme of free, open-air spectator events make St. Augustine's Reach the envy of many other cities and a model for how city waterways can be regenerated.

NARROW QUAY

Narrow Quay, which runs along the eastern side of St. Augustine's Reach, has been progressively restored by the City Council and was opened for public use in 1976. It is now an attractive harbourside walk, much of it pedestrianised in traditional stone setts, with a now well-established avenue of plane trees. Few of the former warehouses survive in what was once the heart of the harbour teeming with merchant ships, and the quayside is now an ideal venue for many of the public events and harbour activities which take place every year.

CABOT

On the quay outside Arnolfini sits the statue of John Cabot, looking over the harbour from which he set out on his famous voyages to America.

Cabot was a Venetian who came to Bristol at the end of the fifteenth century to seek backing for a scheme to explore the western seas—something for which Bristolian merchants had already shown a considerable degree of support.

In May 1497 Cabot set sail from Bristol in the *Mathew* with a crew of 18 or 20 men. On 24 June he reached the coast of North America, stepping ashore at Newfoundland and thus becoming the first known discoverer of America, a year before Columbus reached the southern continent.

TOP LEFT: ST. AUGUSTINE'S REACH DURING ITS FINAL PERIOD AS A COMMERCIAL PORT. MAIN PICTURE: THE *INCA*, ONE OF THE MANY TALL SAILING SHIPS THAT VISIT THE HARBOUR.

Scenes from the harbour regatta, powerboat grand prix and other events—all centred on St. Augustine's Reach. The ferry (top right) links all parts of the harbour throughout the summer season.

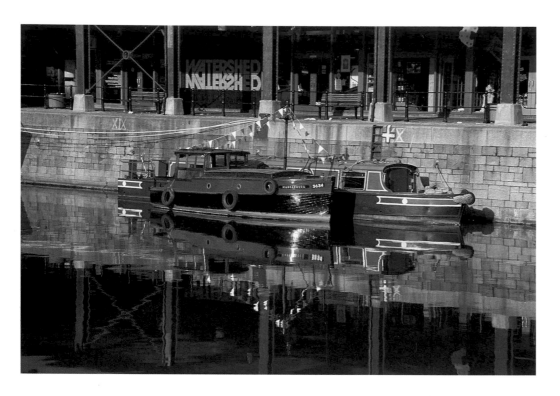

WATERSHED

Watershed Media Centre opened in 1982 as the first centre of its kind in the country, with the aim of providing entertainment and education around the contemporary mass media. Its programme is devoted to contemporary sources of information and entertainment—film, television, video, photography, radio, print and telecommunications.

The centre occupies the first floor of two converted Victorian warehouses overlooking St. Augustine's Reach. The development of the site was the result of a unique collaboration between the City Council, the developers and the Watershed Arts Trust, and has since acted as a model for a number of similar schemes in other cities possessing inner city harbour warehousing in need of imaginative renovation.

Watershed combines cinemas, exhibition space,

photography darkrooms and video production facilities with a large and very popular bar and restaurant, and a profitable conference business. The centre is widely known for its full programme of new British and foreign films and cinema seasons which showcase independent work from this country and abroad. Training courses are run throughout the year in media-related areas like photography, film and video production and sound-recording techniques, and summer schools are organised every year. A regular programme of talks and special events provides a forum for discussion of all aspects of the media.

The conference activities at Watershed include a number of media events and festivals, notably the very popular Wildscreen International Film and Television Wildlife Festival, and the Animation Festival, both of which bring film-makers from all over the world to Bristol.

BRISTOL EXHIBITION CENTRE

Next to Watershed on the western side of St. Augustine's Reach, two nineteenth-century dockside warehouses have been converted to form the Bristol Exhibition Centre. Once a scene of sad neglect, the sheds now play host to a wide range of exhibitions and trade fairs attracting huge attendances throughout the year.

TOP: BOATS MOORED IN ST. AUGUSTINE'S REACH. RIGHT: VIDEO PRODUCTION AT THE WATERSHED. BOTTOM: BRISTOL EXHIBITION CENTRE.

WATERSHED DURING THE HARBOUR REGATTA.

BATHURST BASIN

Bathurst Basin was built on the site of a former millpond as one of three entrances into the floating harbour from the River Avon. In 1872 the original docks on Bathurst Wharf were filled in to create the Bristol Harbour Railway, the first railway in the City Docks. This once-busy commercial dock now retains only two examples of the nineteenth-century Bristol Byzantine-style warehousing that was built all round the area and which became so characteristic of the city. Together with a group of early nineteenth-century cottages and the Smugglers' Tavern, they have been restored and incorporated into Merchants Landing—an attractive new housing development overlooking the water.

The lock into the New Cut was permanently blocked during the Second World War to prevent the emptying of the harbour through bomb damage, and the mechanism of the swingbridge carrying Commercial Road was allowed to decay. Remains of the mechanism and the locks can still be seen, as can the foundations of a bascule bridge which once crossed the junction lock and carried the harbour railway.

By the entrance lock connecting the basin to the main harbour is the Ostrich Inn, a charming late eighteenth-century building which is now a very popular dockside pub with seating on the quayside.

Also overlooking the basin is the Bristol General Hospital, designed between 1855 and 1858 by the same architect who built the two remaining warehouses, W. B. Gingell—one of Bristol's most active and flamboyant Victorian builders. The ground floor of the hospital was built as a warehouse serving the basin.

THE NATIONAL LIFEBOAT MUSEUM

The National Lifeboat Museum houses the world's largest collection of ex-working lifeboats, as well as an extensive selection of photographs, models and artefacts depicting the history of lifeboats and the men who have worked on them over the past 150 years.

Within the museum are two boats which the public can explore inside and out: the 'Maclaughlan', which was stationed at Weston-super-Mare, and the 'North Foreland', featuring a survivors' cabin. Other major exhibits include the 1897 clinker-built 'St Paul' and 'Blue Peter 4', a 16 ft. D class inflatable lifeboat which was one of the original boats paid for by an appeal for old paperbacks on the 'Blue Peter' children's television programme.

TOP: THE OSTRICH, A POPULAR QUAYSIDE INN. BELOW: A SENSITIVE DEVELOPMENT, SUCCESSFULLY BLENDING OLD WITH NEW, IS REFLECTED IN THE WATERS OF THE BATHURST BASIN.

PRINCE'S WHARF

Running west from Prince's Street swingbridge, built in 1879, is Prince's Wharf, now the home of the National Lifeboat Museum and the Bristol Industrial Museum.

Isambard Kingdom Brunel's first great steamship, the *Great Western*, was built and launched there in 1838. This massive wooden-hulled, paddle-driven ship made the very first transatlantic crossing to New York, thus completing Brunel's ambitious project to make a continuous link, via railway and ship, between London and New York.

On the wharf stands the Fairbairn Steam Crane, built by Stothert and Pitt of Bath in 1875, with a lifting capacity of 30 tons. Also built by the same company are the four electric travelling cranes nearby.

TOP DETAIL: AN EARLY ENGRAVING OF THE FAIRBAIRN STEAM CRANE. MAIN PICTURE: WATERCOLOUR OF 1836 SHOWS THE CONSTRUCTION OF THE LEGENDARY S.S. *GREAT WESTERN* AT PRINCE'S WHARF. BELOW: THE NATIONAL LIFEBOAT MUSEUM IS LOCATED IN A REFURBISHED QUAYSIDE WAREHOUSE.

ABOVE: THE INDUSTRIAL MUSEUM IS HOUSED IN DOCKSIDE
TRANSIT SHEDS. BELOW AND RIGHT: THE MARITIME BRISTOL
GALLERY ILLUSTRATES THE HISTORY OF THE PORT.

BRISTOL INDUSTRIAL MUSEUM

Bristol Industrial Museum is housed in dockside transit sheds on Prince's Wharf alongside the Floating Harbour. The museum maintains the technology collections of the City of Bristol Museum and Art Gallery and aims to show something of the immense variety of the industrial work associated with the city.

Transit Sheds 'M' and 'L' were constructed in 1952 replacing the Bristol Corporation Granary destroyed in the Second World War. They were the last to be built in the City Docks and remained in commercial use until the early 1970s. Four electric cranes dating from 1951 are preserved on the quayside; these were used to transfer mixed cargoes between the sheds and vessels. The cargo was sorted inside the sheds and conveyed onto railway wagons and lorries for distribution.

The ground floor of the museum now houses a collection of road and railway vehicles with Bristol associations—indeed, many of them were built in the city. Of particular note are the 'Wanderer' caravan, built in Bristol in 1883 as the world's first touring caravan; the Grenville steam carriage (1875), which is the world's oldest self-propelled passenger vehicle in working order; and the penny-farthing which still holds the world record for 100 miles on a solid-tyred bicycle. There are also numerous interesting horse-drawn vehicles, several Douglas motorcycles, Bristol cars and products of Bristol Commercial Vehicles Ltd., once one of the best bus-building firms in Britain.

The upper floor houses two galleries, one of which is devoted to the story of aircraft engineering in Bristol. The Bristol Aeroplane Co., now two separate companies (Rolls-Royce and British Aerospace), has been responsible for the manufacture of a number of important aircraft and aero-engines. The gallery displays the complete collection of Bristol-built aero-engines, together with a Bristol Sycamore helicopter and a fascinating mock-up of the cockpit of Concorde which was used during the development of the famous supersonic airliner.

ABOVE LEFT: BRISTOL HARBOUR RAILWAY GIVES RIDES ALONG THE QUAYSIDE. ABOVE RIGHT: THE MAYFLOWER PROVIDES TRIPS AROUND THE HARBOUR. LEFT: BRISTOL SYCAMORE HELICOPTER. BELOW: CLASSIC BRISTOL CAR. RIGHT: VEHICLES FROM THE COLLECTION.

In the Maritime Bristol gallery, also on the upper floor, the visitor can find the history of the Port, with many ship-models, reconstructions of workshops and a slave ship, and a viewing gallery giving marvellous views over the harbour. A slide/tape commentary introduces the story and, towards the end, a video describes working in the Port in the words of one of Bristol's dock-crane drivers.

Some of the museum's finest exhibits, which are maintained by volunteers, are to be seen outside the building and are operated regularly (usually at weekends). 'Mayflower', the world's oldest working steam-tug, built in Bristol in 1861, steams frequently during the summer, giving passengers a trip around the docks. Also, locally-built steam locomotives 'Portbury' (1917) and 'Henbury' (1937) are used to operate the Bristol Harbour Railway on regular summer weekends, carrying passengers between the Industrial Museum and the Maritime Heritage Centre near the S.S. *Great Britain*.

The upper floor of 'L' Shed (above the National Lifeboat Museum) houses the reserve collection of the Industrial Museum—some 5,000 objects of all shapes and sizes, representing many local industries. When resources allow, much of this material will be displayed, but for the time being, access is possible by arrangement with the Curator.

THEKLA

The Thekla, now re-christened the Old Profanity Showboat, is a converted freight steamer used as a venue for live entertainment. Built in Germany in 1958 as a cargo-carrying coaster, she sank in 1976 off Rye Harbour. After being salvaged, she was bought by her current owners for conversion to a floating theatre. In 1983 she arrived in Bristol under her own power, and since 1984 has been used for very popular jazz, folk and rock performances as well as occasional theatre and cabaret (below).

GLEVUM

Bristol's revitalised docklands have provided the opportunity for a number of imaginative initiatives around the harbour, among them the use of boats for restaurants and small arts outlets. The Glevum Gallery is situated in the hold of the Bristol-built grain barge 'Glevum', moored at Merchants' Quay.

In 1983 the boat's present owners bought her from Gloucester Docks, where she was due to be scrapped after lying idle for eight years. They opened the Gallery on board in 1984, since when it has become a leading venue for contemporary landscapes and marine paintings by West Country artists.

LOCHIEL

The Lochiel (above), otherwise known as the Inn at the Quay, is one of two floating pubs in the Floating Harbour. Launched in 1939, she carried mail, passengers and cargo on the West Loch Tarbert to Islay run in Scotland until 1970, and was then used for a short time on the Isle of Man route. She was laid-up at Hayle in Cornwall before being bought by Courage (Western) for a floating pub. She was towed to Avonmouth for dry-docking and conversion, and opened in the Floating Harbour in 1978.

YHA BRISTOL CENTRE

14 Narrow Quay, an impressive Edwardian grain warehouse overlooking the harbour next to Bush House, has recently been imaginatively renovated and refurbished as the Youth Hostel Association's Bristol Centre. It also houses Britain's first residential Urban Studies Centre. High-quality budget accommodation is available for all visitors, as well as a varied programme of events and activities about the city. Also in the building are the Bristol Tourist Information Centre and a cafeteria.

LEFT: VINCENT NEEVE, ARTIST AND JOINT OWNER OF THE GLEVUM, WITH ONE OF HIS PAINTINGS. RIGHT: THE GRAIN WAREHOUSE, REFURBISHED AND NOW USED BY THE Y.H.A., WITH A TOURIST INFORMATION CENTRE ON THE GROUND FLOOR.

ARNOLFINI

Arnolfini is Bristol's major centre for the contemporary arts, occupying the two ground floors of one of the city's most handsomely renovated nineteenth-century warehouses. Bush House, originally a tea warehouse dating from the 1830s, stands at the end of Prince Street, at the very heart of the city's harbour complex where the two arms of the floating harbour divide.

Arnolfini has four galleries, a video reference library, an arts, book and record shop and a multi-purpose auditorium for film, music, dance and theatre events. The varied programme of contemporary visual art and live performance events continues Arnolfini's original policy, established when the gallery first opened in small premises in Clifton in 1961, to seek out challenging, often controversial and at times relatively unknown artists and performers and to provide a local, national and international showcase for their work. The galleries not only provide Bristol and the region with exceptional visual arts exhibition spaces for local and regional artists, but offer an ideal venue for large national and international exhibitions of painting, sculpture and photography. Contemporary music performances

range from jazz to classical, and there is an active educational programme providing workshops, talks and events to complement the music and visual arts programmes. The cinema screens new releases and seasons of films from around the world, and the auditorium regularly plays host to the best in contemporary dance.

The popular bar and restaurant was redesigned in 1987 to incorporate original designs by artist Bruce McLean. There are tables outside the building on the quayside, from which visitors can enjoy a splendid view onto the harbour.

TOP: BUSH HOUSE, HOME OF THE ARNOLFINI, DOMINATES THIS AREA OF THE HARBOUR. BOTTOM: NELL NILE, A LOCAL ARTIST FROM ST. PAUL'S, ENJOYED GREAT SUCCESS WITH HER FIRST MAJOR SHOW. LEFT: COMPUTER ART BY WILLIAM LATHAM.

BRISTOL HISTORIC HARBOUR

King Street and
Welsh Back

The eastern end of the harbour skirts the heart of the historic city. Here can be found the oldest continually-active theatre in the country, a seventeenth-century inn whose associations could hardly be more romantic, a splendid square which was once the second largest in Europe and a pub much cherished by jazz buffs. Together with the waterway itself and the partly-cobbled streets, these and other attractions make the King Street/Welsh Back area as rewarding to the visitor as the rest of Bristol's Historic Harbour.

QUEEN SQUARE

Queen Square was named in honour of Queen Anne's visit to Bristol in 1702. When laid out it was the largest open city space in the whole of England after Lincoln's Inn Fields in London. In the middle of the square, which is now somewhat brutally divided by the roadway, stands a statue of William III—widely reckoned to be the best equestrian statue in the country, and cast in 1735/6 by Rysbrack.

The square was conceived at the beginning of the eighteenth century by the newly prosperous and fashion-conscious Bristol corporation as a carefully planned extension of the medieval city into a gracious up-to-date urban residential development. The area chosen was known, aptly, as The Marsh—the promontory south of King Street which was already laid out for walks and recreation.

The leases granted on Queen Square properties laid down sizes and storey heights and stipulated building materials—brick and stone—in the interests of uniformity of design and appearance. The building of the square represented a new way of life in the city; formal gardens, trees and sculpture gave the merchants of Bristol the stylish surroundings which they considered their status and that of the city merited.

Top: autumn colours in Queen Square. Bottom: the Bristol riots of 1831 shook the nation.

Queen Square was at the centre of dramatic events during the Bristol Reform Riots of 1831. The riots were in part the result of long dissatisfaction with the nature of local parliamentary representation and in particular with the opposition by Sir Charles Wetherall, the Recorder of Bristol, to the Reform Bill in the House of Lords. His visit to Bristol to open the Assize Court sparked off two days of the worst urban rioting since the Gordon riots in London 50 years earlier. One of the worst-hit areas was Queen Square, where houses on two sides were burnt down, along with the Mansion House, Excise Office and the Custom House. They were replaced by the slightly Grecian buildings which remain today, including the new Custom House built in 1836.

One of the survivors of earlier times is number 37, where an American consulate was established in 1792, shortly after the American states gained their independence. Also surviving is number 29, the birthplace of Sir Richard Bright, the father of modern kidney treatment.

In the south-east corner of the square is the Hole in the Wall pub, so called after its spyhole, a narrow window at the back of the building reputedly used by locals to keep watch for press-gangs in the eighteenth century. The story goes that the Spyglass in Robert Louis Stevenson's novel *Treasure Island* is based on this inn.

TOP: STATUE OF WILLIAM III BY RYSBRACK. BOTTOM LEFT: BUILDINGS RECENTLY REFURBISHED FOR OFFICE USE. CENTRE RIGHT: NUMBER 29, DATING FROM 1709–11, IS ONE OF THE LEAST-ALTERED OF THE ORIGINAL BUILDINGS IN THE SQUARE. BOTTOM RIGHT: NUMBER 37, IT IS CLAIMED, HOUSED THE FIRST AMERICAN CONSULATE IN ENGLAND.

TOP DETAIL: AN EIGHTEENTH-CENTURY PARISH BOUNDARY MARKER ON THE WALL OF THE BUNCH OF GRAPES. ABOVE: THE LLANDOGER TROW.

CENTRE LEFT: THE LLANDOGER TROW IN THE VICTORIAN PERIOD. CENTRE RIGHT: MERCHANT VENTURERS' ALMSHOUSE. DETAIL TOP RIGHT: THE ARMS OF THE MERCHANT VENTURERS APPEAR ON THE SIDE OF THE BUILDING. BOTTOM LEFT: THE BLUE NOTES JAZZ BAND AT THE OLD DUKE. BOTTOM RIGHT: KING STREET IS WELL PROVIDED WITH PUBS AND RESTAURANTS.

KING STREET

King Street, with its intriguing mixture of architectural styles dating from the seventeenth century to the present, is one of the most attractive and historically interesting streets in Bristol.

The street was laid out in 1663, just outside the medieval city wall, as a row of quality merchants' houses with warehouses to the rear. On one corner is the Merchant Venturers' Almshouse for retired seamen, founded in the fifteenth century, restored in 1699 by Bristol benefactor Edward Colston and still in use. Next door is the Old Library, now a restaurant, built in 1740 as one of the first libraries in the country. Its register of members, kept in the Central Library on College Green, includes the writers Samuel Taylor Coleridge and Robert Southey and the renowned nineteenth-century chemist, Sir Humphry Davy.

The street contains several excellent examples of seventeenth-century timber-frame buildings, the most outstanding being the famous Llandoger Trow pub, The name was taken from the flat-bottomed boats which traded between Bristol and the Welsh coast, and may well refer specifically to the ship of the first publican, a Captain Hawkins, who converted the premises into a public house on his retirement. The pub is reputed to have been the haunt of pirates and the model for the Admiral Benbow in Robert Louis Stevenson's novel *Treasure Island*. It is also said to have been the scene of meetings between writer Daniel Defoe and Alexander Selkirk, the famous castaway who provided the model for Robinson Crusoe.

King Street is well provided with pubs and restaurants. Opposite the Llandoger Trow is Bristol's leading jazz pub, the Old Duke, and the street between the two has been closed to traffic to provide a popular open-air drinking spot in the summer.

Number 33 is another fine example of timber-frame building, with, next to it, a nineteenth-century corn warehouse now refurbished for offices.

St. Nicholas' Almshouse was built in the 1650s on land next to one of the original town gates. A bastion of the thirteenth-century town wall can still be seen in the courtyard.

THEATRE ROYAL

The Theatre Royal in King Street is the oldest theatre in England, with a virtually continuous working history, and is regarded as the country's finest surviving example of a large Georgian town playhouse.

The theatre was opened in 1766 on an unobtrusive plot of land behind Coopers' Hall.

Some elements of the eighteenth-century auditorium still remain: the original wooden gallery benches have been preserved, and the ornate ceiling and intricately carved theatre boxes are much as they would have appeared to the theatre's first audiences. The auditorium itself is horseshoe-shaped, and believed to be the first of this design in the country.

The theatre opened with a gala performance featuring a prologue and epilogue written by the renowned actor David Garrick. Over the next century most of the famous names in British theatre trod its boards, and the ghost of one, Sarah Siddons, is said to tread them still.

The Theatre Royal building was only narrowly rescued from conversion to a factory during the Second World War by the intervention of a group of its trustees. It was leased to the Council for the Encouragement of Music and Arts—the forerunner of the Arts Council—and thereby became the first state theatre in the country. Before long it had resumed its role as a major provincial theatre, and its resident company, the Bristol Old Vic, became one of the country's best known.

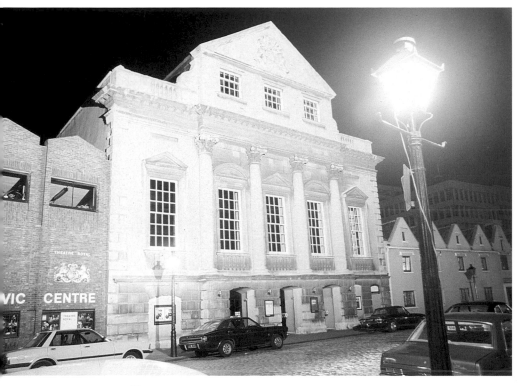

TOP DETAIL: SARAH SIDDONS, WHOSE GHOST IS SAID TO HAUNT THE THEATRE. ABOVE: THE FORMER COOPERS' HALL NOW FORMS THE ENTRANCE. BELOW: THE ORIGINAL AUDITORIUM. BELOW RIGHT: THE STUDIO THEATRE—THE NEW VIC.

A major alteration and extension scheme in 1972 provided new buildings and facilities, incorporating the Coopers' Hall into the entrance foyer and creating a studio theatre—the New Vic—on the site of the previous entrance. As well as seasons of classic drama and new work in both theatres, the building is increasingly used for a range of entertainment and events from music and cabaret to exhibitions and conferences.

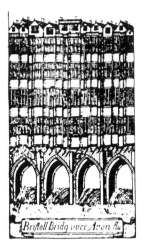

BRISTOL BRIDGE

Bristol derives its name from the Anglo-Saxon 'Bricgstow', meaning settlement by the bridge. Where Bristol Bridge now stands was the very first bridging point into the Saxon settlement, at the junction of the Rivers Avon and Frome. For many years this remained the main entrance and exit for the well-defended burgh inside the encircling rivers.

Originally made of wood, the bridge was rebuilt in stone in the thirteenth century. Like the much larger London Bridge, it had houses on each side of the roadway, many of which had to be rebuilt in 1647 after a fire.

By the mid-eighteenth century, traffic on the bridge was becoming so congested that the corporation had to take drastic measures. The bridge was demolished down to its foundation piers, which were retained for a new triple-arched bridge, built in 1768 to the design of James Bridges after much opposition from the advocates of a single-span bridge. The cast-iron balustrading was added in Victorian times to support the wider road required by even heavier traffic. Four little toll houses on the bridge unfortunately fell victim to this early city centre road-improvement scheme.

ILLUSTRATION AND MAIN PICTURE: BRISTOL BRIDGE TODAY AND AS IT APPEARED IN 1673.

THE LIGHTSHIP

The Lightship, a permanent dockside feature on Welsh Back at the end of King Street, was originally moored off King's Lynn on the East Coast. It has been converted into a restaurant with several bars, and is among the city's most popular harbour haunts, a colourful and unusual focal point for the view down King Street.

WELSH BACK

Welsh back is one of the original quays in the port of Bristol, named for the thriving coastal trade with Wales. Much of the street has been progressively landscaped by the City Council, with the additions of a squash centre and an embarkation point for harbour boat tours on the site of a wartime bomb crater.

LEFT: NEW HARBOURSIDE OFFICE DEVELOPMENT. CENTRE: THE LIGHTSHIP. RIGHT: STONE SETTS AND TREE PLANTING MAKE WELSH BACK A POPULAR PLACE TO RELAX.

ABOVE: BUCHANAN'S WAREHOUSES CONVERTED TO HOUSING.
RIGHT: THE TOWER BELLE DEPARTS FROM WELSH BACK ON A TRIP
UP-RIVER TOWARDS BATH.

WELSH BACK WAREHOUSES

A number of fine Victorian warehouses still stand along the waterfront. Foremost among them, and indeed in the whole country, is the Granary, a superb example of the style that came to be known as 'Bristol Byzantine'. Built in 1871 by leading Bristol industrial architects Ponton and Gough as a grain warehouse, it clearly took its inspiration from the architecture of medieval Italy. A hundred feet high, all seven storeys of its façade are differently decorated with an ingenious variety of brickwork detail.

The opposite side of the water is dominated by three very large and quite outstanding warehouses which are being converted to housing. The two red-brick Buchanan's Warehouses date from 1872, and the W.C.A. Warehouse, built in 1913 by the Western Counties Agricultural Co-operative Association, is one of the earliest examples of the use of reinforced concrete.

COURAGE BREWERY

The Courage Brewery, just over Bristol Bridge, occupies a site which has been a brewing centre for well over two centuries. Originally the Old Porter Brewery, the building was the home of the Bristol Brewery, George's & Co., for more than a century, right up until the Second World War. Many people in Bristol still remember the sight of the superbly-turned-out George's dray horses delivering around the city.

The brewery mainly consists of a conglomeration of Victorian and later buildings rising directly from the water, with the hoist that was once used to haul up sacks of malt and other goods from the river barges still to be seen. The site was quite badly bombed during the Second World War, and has since been much changed and refurbished by Courage's as modernisation of the plant has been carried out. Included in the modernisation was the refurbishment of an attractive terrace of Georgian houses in Bath Street, behind the waterfront. Also renovated was the rather fine former generating station for the Bristol Tramways system, which is now used by Courage's as offices.

LEFT: THE GLASS BOAT IS A SUCCESSFUL FLOATING RESTAURANT
MOORED IN WELSH BACK. CENTRE AND RIGHT: HI-TECHNOLOGY
IS APPLIED TO TRADITIONAL SKILLS AT COURAGE'S BREWERY.

Clifton

The Georgian terraces of Clifton, bordering the spectacular Avon Gorge and rising to Brunel's world-famous Suspension Bridge, present an urban landscape of exceptional elegance and drama. The park and woodland of the Downs, a zoo of international repute and high-quality shops and restaurants within a village atmosphere complete Clifton's unique character.

SUSPENSION BRIDGE

Without a doubt, the Clifton Suspension Bridge is Bristol's most resonant and distinctive landmark. It characterises both the city's historic associations with the great nineteenth-century engineer, Isambard Kingdom Brunel, and its natural advantages—the River Avon flows dramatically along the Gorge beneath, with the Downs on one side and rolling open countryside on the other. A short walk across the bridge takes Bristolians out to the natural beauty of Leigh Woods, the parklands of Ashton Court, and further on to the gentle hills to the south-west of the city.

In 1753 a Bristol wine merchant, William Vick, bequeathed £1,000 at compound interest for a scheme to span the Avon Gorge. By 1829, £8,000 had accumulated, and a competition was held for a design. The young Brunel submitted four designs for a suspension bridge, all with spans greater than any such existing construction. All the entries were rejected by the competition judge Thomas Telford, himself a bridge builder, who was not in the least convinced by Brunel's ambitious and unproven calculations. Telford was then invited to prepare his own design. This, however, met with such little enthusiasm from the bridge committee that they decided to hold a second competition. This time Brunel's design was accepted, and the foundation stone for the bridge was laid in 1831.

The scheme ran into almost immediate financial difficulties, and work did not actually begin until 1836, when a 1,000 ft. long wrought-iron bar was slung across the Gorge to carry a trolley for men and materials. Financial problems continued to dog the project, work was abandoned in 1853, and Brunel himself died in 1859 before he could see his first Bristol design through to completion. The bridge was finally opened on 8 December 1864, five years after his death. It had been somewhat modified since Brunel's original plans; in particular the towers at each end fell sadly short of the ambitious Egyptian-style edifices topped with the sphinxes he had envisaged. The original drawings can be seen in the City Museum. The bridge's final span was 702 ft. 3 in. (213.81 m.) and it is situated 245 ft. (74.62 m.) above high water.

The bridge has over the years given rise to a stock of stories and legends. Sadly, suicides seem irresistibly drawn to it. Most of them do not meet the same unexpected fate that befell Sarah Ann Henley, who in 1885 jumped off—only to be parachuted gently into the mud below by her petticoats. She subsequently lived to the age of 85. Daredevils have leapt off at the end of

Top detail: I. K. Brunel. Illustration: the opening of the bridge as featured on the front cover of the *Illustrated London News*, 17 December 1864.

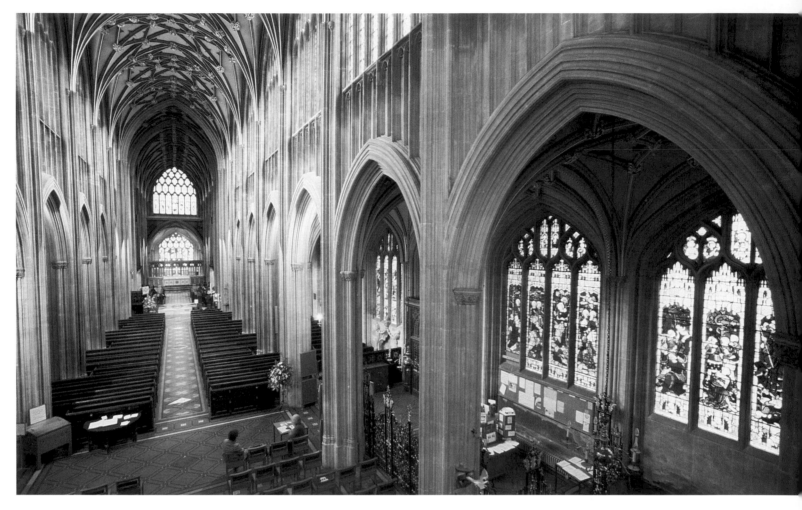

ST. MARY REDCLIFFE

Recognised as perhaps the finest parish church in the country, and reputedly described by Queen Elizabeth I as 'the goodliest, fairest and most famous parish church in England', St. Mary Redcliffe is one of Bristol's jewels.

Built on the red cliffs above the harbour just outside the early city walls, the Church of St. Mary Redcliffe was from the start closely associated with Bristol's seafaring history. It was here that the merchants of the city began and ended their voyages, praying or giving thanks for a good and prosperous passage at the Shrine of Our Lady of Redcliffe, and it is to these same merchants that the city owes the splendour of the church as it is now.

A church has existed on the site since the year 1115, when a church dedicated to 'Blessed Mary of Radclive' was given by Henry I to Salisbury Cathedral. In 1190,

Lord Robert de Berkeley gave his 'Ruge' (ridge) Well in Knowle to the church to supply water to the parishioners of Redcliffe—an event still commemorated in the annual Pipe Walk by the vicar, churchwardens and congregation along the two-mile conduit between the well and the church. A monument in the North Transept

bears an effigy of a crusader knight in full armour believed to be Lord Robert.

The earliest surviving part of the church, the Inner Porch on the north side, dates from about this time. The black pillars are of 'Purbeck marble'—not in fact a marble at all but a hard limestone—shipped from Dorset to Bristol. The present church as we see it was begun towards the end of the thirteenth century, when the upper stage of the tower and the magnificent hexagonal outer porch were built. This porch was the site of the Shrine of Our Lady, and is rare both in its shape and in the quality of its decoration.

Like many medieval churches, St. Mary Redcliffe took shape over many years. In 1446, when work was nearly complete, a violent electrical storm struck the spire which fell and shattered the roof. Repair of the damage and further additions to the church were paid for by wealthy Bristol merchant William Canynges, whose father, William Canynges the elder, had been responsible for much of the preceding work. Canynges

TOP DETAIL: ON GOOD FRIDAY 1941, A GERMAN BOMB LANDED ON REDCLIFFE HILL BLOWING THIS TRAMLINE OVER THE HOUSES AND INTO THE CHURCHYARD. MAIN PICTURE: THE NAVE. BOTTOM: A FINE WOODEN CARVING OF QUEEN ELIZABETH I.

elasticated ropes, pilots have flown beneath it and a number of recent advertisements have featured it against the sunset. The Suspension Bridge exerted a strong fascination over the Victorians who built it, and clearly its appeal endures today.

THE AVON GORGE

The Avon Gorge is a dramatic limestone gorge that creates a stunning natural boundary to the western edge of the city. For many centuries merchant ships brought their cargoes up the tidal River Avon, through the gorge and into the heart of Bristol. The area has inspired many Bristol artists, particularly the nineteenth-century school of Bristol topographical and landscape painters, who would go on sketching parties to the Gorge and Leigh Woods on the other side.

The area is famous for rare trees and flowers, including a white beam, *Bristoliensis*, which grows nowhere else.

The steep cliff-face situated below Clifton Down, and above the busy Portway road, is a favourite spot for rock climbers. In the rock-face can be seen the entrance to St. Vincent's Cave—once only accessible from the cliff outside, but now reached by an underground passage from the Observatory above. The cave may well have been used as a hermitage for the chapel of St. Vincent which is believed to have once perched on the rock. At the city end of the Gorge is Hotwells, once a medicinal hot spring whose virtues were recorded as early as 1480 and which for a time in the eighteenth century came near to rivalling Bath as a fashionable health resort. In the early nineteenth century the water became polluted and the death toll among visiting invalids rose alarmingly. Hotwells went into a decline and many of the spa buildings were demolished, including the Hotwell House and the promontory jutting out into the river on which it stood. All that remains of the once-thriving spa is part of the colonnade alongside the river, next to the modern road.

TOP DETAIL: AN EARLY SCHEME OF 1793 TO SPAN THE AVON GORGE. MAIN PICTURE: THE AVON GORGE VIEWED UP-RIVER TOWARDS THE CITY. ILLUSTRATION BELOW: THE ORIGINAL HOT WELLS. RIGHT: A CLIMBER ON THE ROCK FACE OF THE GORGE.

ABOVE: THE OBSERVATORY HOUSES A CAMERA OBSCURA.
BELOW: THE VAST EXPANSE OF THE DOWNS.

THE OBSERVATORY

The Observatory stands on ground whose history can be traced far further back than that of the city of Bristol itself. Before any settlement was built beside the Avon there was a large Iron Age camp the remains of which can still be seen at the edge of the cliffs on what is now called Observatory Hill.

The base of the Observatory is an old snuff mill which was destroyed in a gale in 1777 and which, for a while, became the site of a beacon intended to be lit in the event of a French invasion during the Napoleonic Wars. In 1828 the Society of Merchant Venturers, who owned the site, granted it at a nominal rent to William West, an artist, for use as a studio. West installed there a quantity of astronomical equipment including, to the enormous interest of the Bristol public, a camera obscura. He also cut an underground passage to St. Vincent's Cave in the rocks below.

The camera obscura is the only piece of equipment remaining from West's large collection of telescopes and astronomical clocks. It has delighted visitors for many years with what was described by the *Bristol Mirror* of the time as 'one of the most extensive and beautiful panoramic views in the kingdom'.

THE DOWNS

Clifton and Durdham Downs provide the city with a very large expanse of open land within minutes of the city centre. So highly valued are the Downs for recreation that they are protected by their own Act of Parliament and uniquely managed by a freestanding committee of city councillors and representatives of the Society of Merchant Venturers.

On winter Saturdays over thirty football pitches are used by the Bristol Downs League, held to be the oldest and largest amateur football league to be accommodated at a single venue in the country.

The Downs are large enough to accommodate football pitches alongside large areas of open space for informal recreation, as well as areas near the Avon Gorge cliff-face which are designated as sites of special scientific interest by the Nature Conservancy Council.

The Downs are the home of the annual Bristol Flower Show, the largest such show in the West Country and still expanding. Held during the week following the August Bank Holiday, the Flower Show caters for every kind of horticultural interest and is an ideal opportunity to see new plant introductions, seek gardening advice, and buy the latest gardening aids.

CLIFF RAILWAY

The Clifton Rocks Railway, running from Hotwells up to the Spa Hotel (later renamed the Avon Gorge Hotel), was built in the 1890s as a result of the self-imposed isolation of the fashionable suburb of Clifton from the rest of the city. The residents of Clifton opposed the construction of any tramways within their district, and the cliff railway was proposed as an answer to the ensuing transport dilemma.

It was unique in the country in that it ran not up the cliff-face but through the rock in a tunnel. Considerable difficulties were encountered in its construction, and it never realised the optimistic forecasts of its potential profitability. It finally closed in 1934, but the lower terminus can still be seen in the cliff-face on the Portway below the Suspension Bridge.

MAIN PICTURE: THE DOWNS ARE THE REGULAR VENUE FOR THE FUNFAIR AND (BOTTOM RIGHT) THE ANNUAL FLOWER SHOW. BOTTOM LEFT: THE CLIFF RAILWAY.

CLIFTON VILLAGE

Up until the eighteenth century, Clifton was a village, separated from the city of Bristol by muddy fields. It comprised no more than a couple of hundred inhabitants and two or three dozen substantial houses set on the edge of an open expanse of heathland.

The eighteenth-century popularity of Hotwells brought more visitors and more building to the lower slopes of Clifton. In the 1780s Clifton Village itself started to expand, beginning with a few gracefully landscaped roads around Boyce's Avenue, followed by The Mall (where the Assembly Rooms were later built at one end) and then spreading down the hill in a positive cascade of magnificent terraces. Unfortunately this enthusiastic building programme was interrupted by the Napoleonic Wars and the crash of 1793, leaving many houses half-built and roofless. Within twenty years, however, Bristol had recovered and the great terraces and crescents on the hillside were all complete. Most splendid of all, 'the crescent to beat all crescents' according to Pevsner, is Royal York Crescent—46 houses overlooking the slopes which fall away to the city's harbour below.

Clifton Village itself—still so-called, perhaps out of a continuing desire to ward off the encroachments of the city—is known particularly for its fashion and antique shops, many of them in the Clifton Antiques Market, and for its plethora of restaurants and wine bars.

A little way from the bustle of the shopping district is Clifton College, founded in 1862 and one of the best-known Victorian public schools. The school still flies the Stars and Stripes on Independence Day in memory of its wartime service as the headquarters of General Omar Bradley, and boasts the highest individual cricket score every made—628 not out, scored by A. E. J. Collins on the college ground in 1899.

CHRISTCHURCH

Christchurch overlooks the Downs at the end of Clifton Down Road and is now, since St. Andrew's was bombed in 1940 and abandoned, the parish church of Clifton. It was started in 1843 by church architect Charles Dyer in the 'Early English' style. It was subsequently added to by a number of architects, notably John Norton, who designed the arcaded and pinnacled tower. The spire is 200 ft. high, and its summit is one of Bristol's highest points above sea level.

ABOVE: ROYAL YORK CRESCENT—THE LONGEST CRESCENT IN EUROPE. BELOW: CHRISTCHURCH.

Scenes from Clifton. Top left: Sion Hill. Top right: Church Walk. Centre left: Clifton Village. Centre right: The Albion. Bottom left: Clifton Antiques Market. Bottom right: Clifton College.

CATHOLIC CATHEDRAL

The Catholic Church of St. Peter and St. Paul (above) was consecrated in June 1973, and is the Roman Catholic Cathedral for the Diocese of Clifton. Its bold, contemporary design by the Percy Thomas Partnership has won many prizes, including the first prize in the 1974 ARIBA competition for the South West region. It has a particularly striking, spacious interior with stained-glass windows by Henry Haig, and is often used to great effect for musical and choral performances.

MANSION HOUSE

Bristol is one of the few cities to have an official residence for its Lord Mayor. This large, imposing house overlooking the Promenade, identified by the coat of arms of the city on the wall, was built in about 1867 and presented to the city by Alderman Thomas Proctor in 1874. It replaced the first mansion house in Queen Square, burnt down in the Reform Riots of 1831, and a house in Great George Street which was used for a short while.

Like Clifton's other 'domestic palaces' (to use the phrase coined by the architectural historian Pevsner) it represents the prosperity of Bristol's nineteenth-century merchant class who had moved away from the city centre to the fashionable 'suburbs'.

GOLDNEY HOUSE AND GARDENS

Thomas Goldney was a wealthy Quaker merchant whose mansion and gardens are one of Clifton's most prized features. In 1720 Goldney, whose interests included a part-share in the privateers which had rescued the famous castaway Alexander Selkirk, moved away from the city centre to Clifton. The fine mansion he built has been very much altered, although the original beautiful mahogany-panelled dining room survives from that time, as does the Orangery, refaced earlier this century.

What makes Goldney House really special, though, are its gardens. These are a work of quite exceptional care and artistry, already famous during the lifetime of their creator, Thomas Goldney's son, another Thomas. The most spectacular feature is the grotto, built over a period of 27 years. The walls and vaults are covered with rock crystal—'Bristol Diamonds'—and thousands of other fantastically shaped shells and fossils which shimmer and sparkle in the light reflected from the nearby cascade. The gardens spread down the slope of the hill in sweeping terraces, incorporating a delightful pool of water lilies and a series of 'fortifications', including a whimsical circular tower topped with battlements and pinnacles. Goldney House is now owned by the University of Bristol. The gardens are opened to the public once a year, and it is well worth seizing the opportunity to see them if at all possible.

LEFT: THE LORD MAYOR'S COACH AND HORSES STANDING OUTSIDE THE MANSION HOUSE. MAIN PICTURE: GOLDNEY GARDENS. ABOVE: THE GROTTO.

BRISTOL ZOO

Bristol Zoo is the fifth oldest zoo in the world, and the city's most popular visitor attraction. It was opened in 1836 by the Bristol, Clifton and West of England Zoological Society on a beautiful 12-acre site on the edge of the Downs. From the start, the gardens were an attraction in their own right. Laid out by the famous landscape gardener Richard Forrest, they contain rare shrubs and trees from all over the world, some splendid display beds and herbaceous borders and one of the best rock gardens in the country.

Like most early zoos, Bristol Zoo was opened with the emphasis on gathering a variety of species together, in the style of a menagerie, and the collection was regularly enlarged by donations from sea captains putting into port in Bristol. In the twentieth century much more importance began to be laid on research and breeding as well as, increasingly, the conservation aspect of the zoo's role. A number of innovative exhibits were introduced, such as an aquarium, a reptile pool and a monkey temple, and in 1954 the zoo's curator, Dr

Richard Clarke, pioneered the world's first nocturnal house, where day and night are reversed.

Bristol Zoo takes pride in its contributions to worldwide breeding programmes which help protect endangered species. Notable 'firsts' for the zoo have included 'Adam'—the first chimpanzee to be successfully reared in Europe—and 'Sebastian'—the polar bear cub, bred in 1958 by a method subsequently adopted worldwide. The quality of the environment in zoos has changed greatly over the past few years, and most of Bristol Zoo's major enclosures have been rebuilt to minimise the use of bars and cages and to create good conditions for breeding and conservation.

A recent, and very popular, addition has been the World of Water, a feat of aquarium engineering which includes five landscaped tanks and the first-ever 'walk-through' aquarium exhibit. The stunning Tropical Bird House, which includes one of the country's largest collections of tropical doves and pigeons, has recently been enlarged and given a glass roof to encourage growth of the plants which are a major feature of the house.

THE ZOO HAS A VERY LARGE COLLECTION OF MAMMALS, BIRDS, FISH AND REPTILES.

97

The Rural City

Bristol is highly unusual and extremely fortunate in having extensive areas of public open space within the city boundary and in close proximity to it. The Downs are described in the previous chapter; here we concentrate on other remarkable oases of greenery.

ASHTON COURT MANSION

The Manor of Ashton is mentioned in Domesday Book and was clearly already a wealthy estate by that time. The mansion, like many houses of its kind, has had a complex architectural history over the centuries in which its wealthy landowning inhabitants have 'modernised' and enlarged it.

The first owners were the de Lyons family from France. The house in which they lived was a simple medieval manor house, far smaller than the present building. In 1454 the manor was sold to Richard Choke of Stanton Drew—later Sir Richard Choke, the famous Justice of Common Pleas—who enlarged the house greatly and generally embellished it as befitted his station in life.

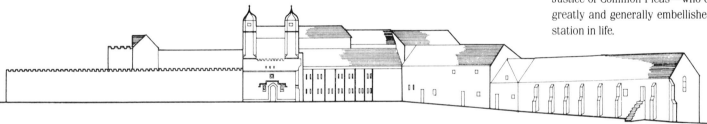

The house then passed through several hands before being bought in 1545 by wealthy Bristol merchant John Smyth. He probably never actually lived in the manor but used it as a suitable place for entertaining his fellow merchants. However, his son, Hugh, took up residence there on his marriage, and for the next four centuries Ashton Court was the home of the descendants of the Smyth family.

Although earlier parts of the building still exist, it was the Smyths who created the house we see today. In 1633 Thomas Smyth, M.P., built a new south façade which was clearly influenced—although not designed, as some early records hopefully claimed—by the successful architect Inigo Jones. This façade remained substantially unaltered during subsequent additions and renovations, and survives more or less unchanged today.

TOP: MAIN ENTRANCE TO THE MANSION. TOP RIGHT: DETAIL FROM THE MONUMENT TO SIR RICHARD CHOKE AND HIS WIFE IN LONG ASHTON PARISH CHURCH. CENTRE: THE HOUSE IN THE EARLY TUDOR PERIOD. BOTTOM: THIS DRAWING BY BONNER SHOWS THE HOUSE AFTER THE ADDITION OF THE NEW WING IN 1633.

During the eighteenth century the Smyth family fortunes declined and the bulk of the estate passed to Jarrit Smith, an eminent Bristol attorney and later M.P. for the city, who had married into the family. He obtained a grant to bear the Smyth arms, and his children took their mother's name, thus keeping the estate in the family name.

Further additions to the house were made by succeeding heirs, and it was not until the 1950s that the house finally passed out of the family's ownership. In 1959 it was acquired by Bristol City Council, together with the park, as a public amenity for the enjoyment of the people of Bristol. Although the park has for many years been an extremely popular and well-used open space, the mansion lay in sad neglect for some time. It has been gradually renovated by the City Council and used for conferences and banquets, and is now being developed as a genuine leisure amenity after public consultation about its use.

TOP: A PHOTOGRAPH TAKEN IN THE MUSIC ROOM IN THE 1920s CAPTURES A LIFESTYLE LITTLE CHANGED SINCE THE VICTORIAN ERA. BOTTOM: THE MUSIC ROOM TODAY. TOP RIGHT: MUCH OF THE INTERIOR IS STILL DERELICT, BUT THE CITY COUNCIL IS DETERMINED TO CONTINUE THE RESTORATION. BELOW RIGHT: THE MAGNIFICENT VAULTED HALL.

ASHTON COURT ESTATE

Ashton Court was acquired by the City Council in 1959 and opened to the public in 1960 to become one of the nation's largest and most popular parks. Only two miles from the city centre, the near-1,000 acre estate plays host to an impressive calendar of events throughout the year.

Ashton Court is the home of the North Somerset Show, whose use of the park dates back to the private ownership of the Smyths. More recently, the park has proved to be the ideal launch-site for hot-air balloons. Bristol is the home of the world's largest balloon manufacturer and Ashton Court provides the setting for the International Balloon Fiesta, the sixth-largest outdoor event in the United Kingdom and the largest hot-air balloon meeting outside of America.

As well as a succession of popular events including Senior Citizens' Day—an event still unique to Bristol—Ashton Court has many permanent attractions, such as the two approach-and-putt golf courses, a nature trail and this country's first permanent orienteering trail. It is the home of SORCY, the Self-Organised Riding Club for Youngsters, and of the Bristol Society for Model and Experimental Engineers, whose track for model locomotives is one of the longest and best in the country.

The estate is an historic landscape and includes the remains of an ancient oak forest. One notable survivor is the famous Domesday Oak. Now buttressed and braced, the gnarled trunk and branches of this ancient tree, believed to be at least 600 years old, support a mass of fresh green foliage and a healthy crop of acorns every year.

Sir Hugh Smyth, who inherited the estate in 1802, went ahead with alterations to Ashton Court and a replanning of the parkland. The park wall, built in his time, is five miles in length. This was the era of landscaping the great estates. Reshaping and replanting, especially with the new varieties of trees and shrubs that were being found in North America, was extremely fashionable. Sir Hugh was advised by the eminent landscape architect of the period, Humphry Repton. A plan of the park was drawn when the work was completed in 1826; this plan, which is in the City Record Office, shows the parkland very much as it is today.

Although red and fallow deer have been enclosed in the park since the fourteenth century, their reintroduction was made possible during World Wildlife Year in 1970. The herd is particularly fine and very popular with the thousands of visitors who come to enjoy the many delights of the city's greatest leisure asset.

TOP DETAIL: STAG FROM THE ESTATE HERD. LEFT: THE TRANQUIL SETTING OF CHURCH WOOD. RIGHT: CATTLE JUDGING AT THE NORTH SOMERSET SHOW.

MAIN PICTURE: THE SPECTACULAR ANNUAL INTERNATIONAL
BALLOON FIESTA. LEFT: SHOW JUMPING AT THE NORTH SOMERSET
SHOW. ABOVE: THE ANNUAL BRISTOL–BOURNEMOUTH VINTAGE
CAR RALLY ATTRACTS MANY ENTRANTS. RIGHT: THE UNIQUE
SENIOR CITIZENS' DAY

LEIGH WOODS

There are few cities lucky enough to have the kind of woodland scenery that Bristol possesses so near its city centre. Leigh Woods, just across the Suspension Bridge from Clifton, is an area of quiet, informal beauty, where paths suddenly open out onto spectacular views over the Avon Gorge hundreds of feet below.

The woods are owned by the National Trust and managed by the Nature Conservancy Council as the Avon Gorge National Nature Reserve. The well-marked paths offer walks of varying lengths, and there are several sites of old hillforts on the high ground overlooking the river.

Stoke Leigh Woods to the west, entered through a splendid Greek Revival gateway which once led to Leigh Court Mansion, belong to the Forestry Commission and are also laid out in attractive walks.

ARNO'S VALE CEMETERY

There is a local tradition that the name Arno's Vale may derive from the valley of the River Arno in Florence, said to have inspired some of the more Gothic extravagances of its landowners. It is, however, more likely to have originated, rather more prosaically, from an early landowner by the name of Arno.

The area must once have been a quite delightful spot on the edge of Bristol. With two great houses and large tracts of parkland, Arno's Court Estate was created in the 1760s for the rich and eccentric Bristol merchant William Reeve. The realisation of Gothic fantasies such as a fake medieval gateway, bath-house and colonnade, and splendid black castle made out of the slag waste from his brass foundries ultimately proved to be his financial ruin. These delightfully idiosyncratic edifices have lost most of their collective effect now that road-

widening schemes have cut a swath through the estate.

The site on which Arno's Vale Cemetery now stands was once the location of a Georgian mansion, Arno's Vale House, whose estate covered 40 acres. It was the home of John Cave, a wealthy Bristol banker and one-time partner in the Phoenix Glassworks.

The first portion of the cemetery was consecrated in 1840 in a ceremony that attracted a large and admiring crowd who felt, according to the *Bristol Journal* of the day, that 'few, if any, cemeteries in the Kingdom will surpass that of Bristol'.

Among the nineteenth-century Christian tombs and gravestones is an Indian-style mausoleum, the burial place of one of Bristol's most intriguing, if short-term, inhabitants, Raja Rammohun Roy. Born in about 1774 in Bengal, Rammohun Roy was a well-to-do and highly educated Brahmin who had served in the East India Company before becoming a writer, social reformer and educational pioneer. He was sent as an envoy to England

in 1831, and came to Bristol in 1833. Unfortunately, only ten days after his arrival he contracted meningitis and died shortly afterwards. His remains were ultimately re-interred in a mausoleum in Arno's Vale cemetery. Designed by the grandfather of the poet Tagore, it is now the object of an annual pilgrimage by many people of Indian origin.

FROME VALLEY

The River Frome rises in Dodington Park on the lower slopes of the Cotswolds and pursues a winding course to the historic harbour in the city centre. The river is at its most attractive where it is contained in a valley of continuous parkland between Oldbury Court Estate on the city's north-east boundary and Eastville Park.

Oldbury Court is a major city park and former home

of the Vassall family. The River Frome plunges over several weirs until it reaches the pretty Snuff Mills Park. The old mill has been partly restored, although its name is derived from the nickname of its one-time owner, 'Snuffy Jack', rather than its purpose. Indeed, the flow of water was insufficient to drive the mill and the remains of a large, early industrial boiler have been uncovered for public display.

The river continues its journey through the attractive Wickham Glen to emerge alongside Eastville Park, originally known as the People's Park and the first home of the Bristol Rovers Football Club. The park remains popular for soccer and for its man-made lake which lies above the level of the Frome.

Bristol is fortunate in having such a beautiful, two-and-a-half-mile countryside walk so close to the centre of the city. A nature trail and guide is available, providing information about the valley's earlier history and its present-day abundance of wildlife.

furnishings and farm and craft tools. Repton's Red Book for Blaise, which outlined his scheme, and archaeological material excavated within the grounds are also on display. A finely detailed model of the hamlet forms the centrepiece of a permanent

exhibition on the history of the estate and its mansion. The museum also houses a specialist library and archives which may be consulted by appointment. Other activities provided by the museum include work with schools, public lectures and, in the summer, demonstrations of traditional butter-making which take place in John Nash's dairy. Admission to the hamlet, estate and museum is free.

Nearby, in St. Mary's Churchyard, Henbury, stands the grave of Scipio Africanus, a black slave who died in Bristol in 1720 at the age of 18. The young man, named after the Roman general who defeated Hannibal in 202 B.C., had been in the service of the Earl of Suffolk and his wife, who had clearly been fond enough of him to provide him with a dignified burial place and touching memorial. The gravestone records that Scipio had become a Christian, and suggests that he had been released from slavery before his death.

BLAISE CASTLE ESTATE

For over half a century, citizens and visitors have been able to enjoy Blaise Castle Estate as a public park. The estate forms part of a ridge of open space to the north-west of the city whose fine landscape includes Kingsweston Down and Penpole Woods. The castle from which the park takes its name is a Gothic folly built in 1766 standing on an ancient Iron Age hillfort which is now a scheduled ancient monument.

BLAISE CASTLE HOUSE MUSEUM

Blaise Castle House was built by the Bristol architect William Paty in 1796 for John Scandrett Harford, a prosperous Bristol merchant and banker. Harford also employed Humphry Repton, famous for his picturesque interpretation of landscape gardening, to improve the grounds. Repton's design, which included the impressive carriage drive from the house to the castellated entrance in Henbury Road, largely established the present-day appearance of the estate. Repton introduced Harford to the eminent architect John Nash, who added a thatched dairy, a conservatory and the much-celebrated Blaise Hamlet to the estate. Completed in 1812, the nine cottages which make up Blaise Hamlet were built to house the retired servants of the Harfords. It is now owned by the National Trust.

Blaise Castle House Museum, which opened in 1949 holds the social history collections of the City Museum and Art Gallery. The museum contains displays representing many aspects of everyday life in the Bristol area over the past 300 years. Especially noteworthy are the textiles, costumes, toys, domestic

MAIN PICTURE: BLAISE HAMLET. TOP RIGHT: BLAISE HOUSE. BOTTOM RIGHT: THE GRAVE OF SCIPIO AFRICANUS IN ST. MARY'S CHURCHYARD, HENBURY.

105

Coast and
Countryside

As this book shows, Bristol has numerous places of interest and beauty for residents and visitors to enjoy. It is also a perfect base from which to discover much of the finest countryside in England and South Wales. The character of the region is too subtle and elusive to be captured in the following account of some of its individual features. Only through exploration—over a day, a weekend or in the course of a lifetime—will its true flavour emerge.

AMERICAN MUSEUM

The neoclassical manor house on the top of the hill at Claverton, just outside Bath, was designed in 1820 by Sir Jeffery Wyatville, architect to King George IV. It has two major claims to fame: on 26 July 1897 Winston Churchill delivered his first political speech there, and on 1 July 1961 it opened as Europe's only comprehensive museum of Americana.

The interior of the house has been cleverly reconstructed into rooms authentically furnished to represent different periods in North American history. Many of the fittings were brought over from houses in the United States, as was all the beautifully crafted furniture. The effect is both to display an impressive range of American crafts and skills and to create a fascinating picture of domestic life over the centuries since the first colonists arrived on American soil.

Visitors begin with the Keeping Room, constructed with beams and floorboards from a seventeenth-century Massachusetts house, which gives an idea of what the home of a Puritan New England family of the time might have looked like. Other rooms illustrate the lifestyles of different kinds of Americans in the eighteenth and nineteenth centuries and the skills which went into furnishing and decorating their homes. The museum has a wonderful collection of quilts, rugs and textiles and beautiful examples of stencilling and other early decorative crafts.

In the grounds is an American herb garden and a replica of George Washington's garden at Mount Vernon—the original having been planted with seeds sent out to him by the Fairfax family of Writhlington, near Bath.

Before leaving the museum, most visitors make time to call in at the Country Store and the herb shop on the terrace, and to enjoy the delicious home-baked cakes and cookies in the tea rooms.

AVEBURY

The little Wiltshire village of Avebury has the unique distinction of being set in the centre of one of the most spectacular prehistoric stone and earth rings in Europe. This takes the form of an enormous bank and ditch surrounding most of the village, with a series of stone circles within it. The full extent and original form of the standing stones is now difficult to gauge, as many were broken up over the years. In fact it was not until an interest was shown by the seventeenth-century antiquarian and essayist John Aubrey that the site was acknowledged as important.

Some of the stones from the mysterious prehistoric circles are actually embedded in the walls of the cottages on the main street of the village. Much fascinating information about this and other nearby prehistoric sites is provided by the Alexander Keiller Museum. Situated in the middle of the village, this museum was founded in about 1938 and named after the man who was Avebury's chief archaeologist.

The pleasant Elizabethan manor house is open to the public, and contains some fine panelled rooms and plasterwork ceilings. The formal gardens are distinguished by some interesting topiary work.

Pretty though the village is, the real fascination of Avebury is the extraordinary way in which centuries of history are telescoped into such a small place; the monuments of prehistory providing a background for the rural charm of seventeenth-century village England.

BADMINTON HOUSE

Badminton House in Gloucestershire is a very fine example of Palladian architecture, a style much favoured by the English landed gentry. It has been the home of the Dukes of Beaufort since the seventeenth century, and has within its walls beautiful collections of Italian, Dutch and English paintings. The game of badminton was invented in the large entrance hall to the house, which is why all original courts were built to the dimensions of this hall.

Badminton is also internationally famous for its three-day horse trials held in April every year.

TOP: AVEBURY. LEFT: THE AMERICAN MUSEUM, NEAR BATH. RIGHT: BADMINTON HORSE TRIALS.

BATH

The history of Bath begins in legend, with the story of the discovery of healing waters by the ancient Britons and the founding of a sacred spa. Legend turns into established archaeological fact with the arrival of the Romans, who created a spa which by the third century became a centre for visitors from all over the Roman world. With the pragmatic compromise of an occupying force they incorporated the name of a local Celtic goddess (Sulis Minerva) into the name of their splendid new city (Aquae Sulis) and created a series of public buildings and bathing establishments with the temple of Sulis Minerva at their centre.

After four centuries of busy life, Roman Bath collapsed, almost literally, into the marsh. Its fortunes revived somewhat under the Saxons, and King Edgar was crowned there in 973 in a ceremony which established a model for subsequent coronations in this country. In Norman times the city was dominated by the great Abbey and surrounding monastic buildings which became the diocesan cathedral when the Bishop of Wells transferred the seat to Bath. It was not until 1243 that Wells was reinstated and the see became Bath and Wells, as it is today.

Later bishops favoured Wells—whose importance grew at the expense of Bath—and the fabric of the cathedral decayed, along with the prosperity of the town. The rebuilding of the cathedral was started in the sixteenth century, helped along by a national appeal by Queen Elizabeth I. Although the reputation of its spring waters had never completely faded and visitors still came in search of cures to a staggering range of ailments, Bath was, in 1622, described by its mayor as 'a verie little poor Citie', its cloth-making industry much declined and its economy struggling.

All was to change soon, however. In the early years of the eighteenth century the energy of a handful of architects and a few arbiters of social taste transformed Bath into the most fashionable watering place in the

country. The social style of the city was set by Richard ('Beau') Nash; its architectural development by John Wood the Elder. This architect and amateur antiquarian dreamed of re-creating the glory of Roman Bath throughout the city, and his designs for Queen Square (1728–36), the Parades (1740–3) and the Circus (1754) began the extraordinary spate of Georgian building that created the elegance and charm that characterise the city today. The younger Wood built Royal Crescent between 1767 and 1775, whilst Robert Adam's Pulteney Bridge opened the way for Thomas Baldwin's Great Pulteney Street, leading to the suburb of Bathwick. Entertainment for the influx of wealthy and fashionable visitors was provided in the new Pump Room, Assembly Rooms and Guildhall, and for some years Bath reigned supreme as the focus for London's socialites when they left the capital. Fun can be had spotting the many plaques marking the houses where famous visitors lodged or lived.

Bath today is by no means the lifeless museum that such a heritage might suggest. There is a rich cultural life in the city, culminating every year in the Bath International Festival, and it has also won many awards for its stunning floral displays. In addition Bath is renowned for its shopping, and with its indoor markets, narrow lanes lined with shops, cafés and restaurants, and pedestrianised shopping precincts it offers an embarrassment of choice to tourists and residents alike.

MAIN PICTURE: BATH ABBEY. LEFT: PULTENEY BRIDGE AND
THE RIVER AVON.

BERKELEY CASTLE

Berkeley Castle is set in pretty countryside in the town of Berkeley, just off the A38 between Bristol and Gloucester. It is highly unusual in having retained many elements of its early existence as a fortified castle whilst developing over the centuries into a family home.

It was built 800 years ago by the Berkeley family, and its medieval walls and dungeons are still in evidence. One of the murkier moments in Berkeley's early history was King Edward II's imprisonment and subsequent brutal murder in one of the cells on the orders of his wife.

Over the years the fortified stronghold was gradually transformed into a family home, and the splendidly furnished rooms bear witness to the status and wealth of its aristocratic and influential owners. The grounds contain a deer park and butterfly house which are well worth seeing.

BIBURY

Bibury was described by nineteenth-century artist William Morris as the most beautiful village in England. Even allowing for the intrusions of twentieth-century tourism, it certainly is an exquisite example of Cotswold village England.

Bibury's most immediately noticeable feature is a broad stream running through the middle of the village. Crammed with large trout, it is a source of great interest to the many visitors throughout the year.

Most of the village is built in warm Cotswold stone, seen at its most attractive in Arlington Row, a beautifully preserved collection of seventeenth-century weavers' cottages, now owned by the National Trust. On the bridge nearby, Arlington Mill, once a corn mill, is now a country museum housing a collection of agricultural implements, photographs and a Victorian printing press. Bibury Court, superbly positioned on the river, is a stately Jacobean mansion, once the home of the Sackville family.

Instead of a village green, Bibury—somewhat unusually—has a village swamp. Known as Rack Isle, this now serves as a wildfowl reserve inhabited by large numbers of ducks and geese.

CHEW VALLEY AND BLAGDON

The Chew Valley, just to the north of the Mendip Hills, has some of the prettiest and least-spoilt countryside and villages within easy reach of Bristol. Chew Valley lake, which was created in 1955 as a reservoir for the Bristol area over the site of Roman settlements and a medieval village, is a popular spot for fishing, boating and picnicking.

Nearby Blagdon also has a lake which was made by damming the river Yeo. Both lakes are well-stocked with trout from the hatchery at Ubley which lies between them. A very fine church, with a good deal of its original Norman detail still remaining, can also be found at Blagdon.

BOWOOD HOUSE

Bowood House near Calne in Wiltshire has been the family home of the Earls of Shelburne since 1754. Much of the house is open to visitors, as are the beautiful and extensive grounds.

Robert Adam was the principal architect of the house, which has been restored to its Georgian proportions by alterations and renovations carried out quite recently. Among the rooms open to the public are a magnificent Adam library housing some 5,000 volumes, the laboratory in which Dr Joseph Priestley discovered oxygen in 1774, and a fine Victorian chapel. The Orangery was turned into a picture gallery by the present earl's father, and a newly-converted sculpture gallery contains the remainder of the famous Lansdown Sculptures.

A fascinating version of England's social history seen from the viewpoint of one of its privileged families is presented in a series of rooms containing family memorabilia. These include such curiosities as Lord Byron's Albanian costume and Queen Victoria's wedding chair. A large and intriguing collection of objects from India dates from the time of the present earl's grandfather, who was viceroy there between 1888 and 1894.

Bowood is particularly well-known for its gardens and parklands, which were landscaped by England's most famous gardener, Capability Brown, between 1762 and 1768. Terraces, a lake, a Doric temple, cascades and grottoes provide an exquisite setting for year-round displays of colour. Nearly 200 types of trees and shrubs are collected in the arboretum, whilst two miles from the house there are separate rhododendron gardens which are a huge attraction during the early summer. For children, a large adventure playground in the park, complete with rope-ladders, tree-cabins and a pirate galleon, offers an experience not to be forgotten.

LEFT: BERKELEY CASTLE. TOP CENTRE: BIBURY—RACK ISLE AND ARLINGTON ROW. BOTTOM: BLAGDON. RIGHT: BOWOOD HOUSE.

BURRINGTON COMBE AND ROCK OF AGES

Burrington Combe, a hillside valley cut into the north slopes of the Mendip Hills, has several caverns in its limestone rockface which are much visited by cavers. Less spectacular than Cheddar Gorge, and consequently less commercialised, the combe has a different and rather quieter appeal. Abandoned limestone quarries provide convenient car parks and good starting points for the paths up the steep-sided valley. These lead to some excellent long walks on the very top of Mendip ridge and a rewarding view right across to the Bristol Channel. At the foot of the Valley, and marked by a plaque, is the Rock of Ages, where the Reverend A. Toplady sheltered from a storm and was inspired to compose the well-known hymn of that name.

CASTLE COMBE

Only fragments remain of the Norman castle from which this beautiful little village, set deep into a wooded Wiltshire valley, takes its name. But there is still a great deal of history to be seen in the mellow stones of Castle Combe.

An important weaving centre in the fifteenth century, the village still contains a row of weavers' cottages from that era in Water Lane. There is also a church in which can be found the thirteenth-century tomb and effigy of Walter de Dunstanville, who owned the manor after the Norman Conquest. Castle Combe was once designated the prettiest English village, and its atmosphere of quaint charm is irresistible, if a little too carefully nurtured for complete enchantment. This appeal has much to do with the effect of its collection of gabled and mossy-roofed Cotswold-stone cottages pressing higgledy-piggledy onto the narrow streets.

A brook runs through the village beneath the triple-arched bridge on the main street, and a canopied market cross stands in the village square. The seventeeth-century manor house which once belonged to the Scrope family—lords of the manor for 500 years—is now an excellent hotel and restaurant. The village was once used for filming part of *Dr Doolittle*, but oddly enough masqueraded as a fishing port for the film.

Nearby is the famous Castle Combe motor racing circuit.

CHEDDAR

Cheddar, the village that gave its name to England's most popular cheese, is one of the West Country's most prized beauty spots, and, it must be said, suffers for it in terms of tourists per square inch.

The village itself was important in Saxon times as the site of a royal palace, a centre of religion and a productive farming area—a reputation which survives in the fame of its strawberries. The cliffs of the gorge were for many years a great attraction and a point of great interest for botanists and geologists, but it was with the discovery of the caves in the gorge in the nineteenth century that the area became a real tourist spot. The first cave was opened up in 1837, and named after its discoverer, Cox, who reputedly happened upon it whilst hacking away at the rock-face to make room for a new cart shed. Gough's cave was opened up 40 years later, and together they now form the nucleus of a busy tourist centre. They are well worth visiting for their spectacular stalactite formations, as well as for the successful way in which the displays exploit contemporary technology in the form of light shows and holograms.

The gorge itself is a wonderful place to walk, with its intriguing rock formations, dramatic scenery and rare plants such as the Cheddar pink. Paths and nature trails lead up to the top of Mendip, where walkers can enjoy views over the countryside to the Bristol Channel.

TOP LEFT: CASTLE COMBE. TOP RIGHT: CHEDDAR GORGE. LEFT: THE ROCK OF AGES WITH ITS FAMOUS CLEFT WHERE THE REVEREND TOPLADY SHELTERED.

111

ABOVE: CHEPSTOW CASTLE AND THE RIVER WYE. BELOW: CIRENCESTER.

CHEPSTOW CASTLE

Chepstow Castle, now in rather dramatic and sombre ruins, was one of the first castles to be built by the Normans after the Conquest, and was still partly habitable at the beginning of the nineteenth century.

It was built by the Norman lord, William fitz Osbern, and served both as a defensive bastion and as a base for his advance into Wales. The Great Tower, roofless and floorless today, is the most impressive relic of this time. The Great Gatehouse—the present main entrance—was built in the thirteenth century together with a number of other additions which have not withstood the years quite as well as the massive walls of the Great Tower.

Like most castles, Chepstow has had its share of prisoners, including Edward II, who spent six days there before his removal to Berkeley Castle in Gloucestershire. Henry Marten, an extreme anti-royalist was also held there for twenty years after the Restoration in the tower now known as Marten's Tower.

With its commanding position on the hill guarding the river approach to the town, the castle is an impressive reminder of the turbulent history of the Welsh Marches.

CIRENCESTER

Cirencester was the second largest city in Roman Britain, and stands at the junction of several ancient roads. Fittingly, the town possesses one of the country's finest collections of Roman antiquities, housed in the Corinium Museum. Exhibits include some very fine floor mosaics and a Roman kitchen complete with menu for a lavish dinner party—dormice a speciality.

These days it is a bustling and yet relaxed town centred around its busy marketplace where a thriving street market is still held. The marketplace is dominated by an imposing church whose fifteenth-century tower contains the oldest ring of twelve bells in the country. The very beautiful porch was built in 1500, and the sumptuous interior is a testament to the prosperity of the wool trade in the region at the time.

Just down the road from the marketplace is the massive 36 ft. yew hedge of Cirencester Park, home of Lord Bathurst. The house itself is not open to the public but the estate's 3,000 acres of public parkland offer wonderful landscaped walks, woodlands, a model farm and polo matches in the summer.

ABOVE: CLEVEDON PIER COLLAPSED IN A STORM IN 1970 AND IS NOW FINALLY BEING REPAIRED AND RESTORED. BELOW: DRAMATIC OPEN SPACE ON THE COTSWOLDS.

CLEVEDON

Clevedon is one of those British seaside resorts whose large, Victorian Italianate houses, tree-lined cliff walks and carefully laid out little parks bear witness to a turn-of-the-century heyday now long past. Between 1820 and 1900 the town's population grew tenfold, and it acquired an elegant iron pier and a broad esplanade where fashionable crowds would gather in the evenings to enjoy the music coming from the bandstand. Much of this development came about through the energy of Sir Arthur Hallam Elton.

The late Norman church contains a memorial to the poet Tennyson's dear friend Arthur Hallam, an earlier member of the prominent local family, whose death in 1833 inspired the famous poem *In Memoriam*. Also honoured in the church are the Elton family who for many years lived at Clevedon Court two miles away. This attractive and unostentatious fourteenth-century manor house is now owned by the National Trust and open to visitors. The house has a chapel with two unique windows of reticulated tracery, and a fine collection of Nailsea glass and Elton Ware pottery, made famous by Sir Arthur Hallam Elton's son Edmund—the 'potter baronet'. Examples of his internationally known work can be seen on the clock tower built to celebrate Queen Victoria's Diamond Jubilee.

THE COTSWOLDS

The Cotswolds is one of Britain's official 'Areas of Outstanding Natural Beauty', and in the gentle, human scale of its charm provides a happy counterpoint to some of the more dramatic and awe-inspiring beauty spots in other parts of the country. It is a landscape of villages and domestic architecture whose quiet appeal lies both in the unhurried pace of village life and in the warmth of the characteristic pale-golden Cotswold stone.

The wealth of the Cotswolds grew hugely when it became the centre of the English wool trade in the Middle Ages. Fortunes were made from the industry, and were spent on local buildings, particularly on the endowment of churches—these 'wool churches' are to be found all over the area.

The Cotswolds suffered enormously with the decline of the wool trade, and poverty struck deep. Ironically, it was this very poverty that prevented further development and thus preserved the rural charm that has made the area the great tourist attraction it is today.

CORSHAM COURT

The manor house of Corsham Court in Wiltshire is one of the oldest in the county. Dating in part from the thirteenth century, it has been continuously lived in for nearly seven hundred years. The present building dates largely from Elizabethan times, and is the work of Thomas Smyth. It was bought by the Methuen family in 1745 and, although much extended and remodelled by later architects, it has kept its overall Elizabethan character.

Former owners of the house were passionate collectors of art, and Corsham contains an exceptional collection of sixteenth- and seventeenth-century old masters, and a famous collection of English furniture, including Chippendale and Adams.

The park was landscaped in the 1760s by Capability Brown and later by Sir Humphry Repton.

DEVIZES

Named in Norman times for the meeting of boundaries it marked, Devizes began as a castle town and grew steadily into the thriving market town it continues to be—busy but not rushed; pleasantly out of the way without being sleepy.

The first castle, built in the twelfth century, fell into ruins in the sixteenth century and its stones were used to build houses in the town. The present 'castle' dates from Victorian times.

The town of the Middle Ages can still be glimpsed in a number of timber-frame houses and several very fine churches. Larger houses testify to the prosperity of the town in the eighteenth century. The Bear Hotel was a coaching stop at this time, and sheltered many famous visitors including the infamous Judge Jeffreys, the scourge of the West Country.

DUNTISBOURNE LEER AND DUNTISBOURNE ROUS

The Duntisbourne valley in Gloucestershire contains some of the prettiest, least-spoilt and most characteristic villages in the Cotswolds, harbouring in their quiet seclusion some rare examples of early church architecture.

Duntisbourne Leer is a tiny village, scarcely more than a hamlet, made up of a collection of high barns, Cotswold-stone cottages and picture-book gardens. The road through the village runs through an ancient ford, often occupied by the village ducks.

Duntisbourne Rous nestles in a deep hollow, with a tiny and exceptionally beautiful Saxon church perched above the village on the steep slope of the valley. It is unusual for a village church in that it has a crypt in which there is a small Norman east window.

TOP LEFT: CORSHAM COURT AND TOP DETAIL: MICHELANGELO SCULPTURE ON DISPLAY. TOP RIGHT: DEVIZES TOWN CENTRE. BOTTOM LEFT: DUNTISBOURNE LEER AND BOTTOM RIGHT: DUNTISBOURNE ROUS.

DOLEBURY HILLFORT

During the Iron Age the countryside that is now Somerset and Avon was occupied by the Dobunni tribe whose social, economic and military organisation was quite sophisticated. The landscape still bears the signs of many hillforts from this time, one of the most impressive being Dolebury Camp on the edge of the Mendips, not far from the town of Churchill. The location of the camp suggests it was a key point in the defence of the Mendip passes.

DYRHAM PARK

Dyrham, just north of Bath, is the site of one of the most significant battles of the Saxon invasion of Britain. In 577, two Saxon leaders defeated three British kings there, captured their cities of Bath, Gloucester and Cirencester and pushed the defending Britons west into Wales.

The name is an ancient one meaning 'deer enclosure', and has been given renewed significance by the herd of fallow deer that now grazes the rolling acres of Dyrham Park, a large house and parkland in the ownership of the National Trust and open to the public.

The mansion, which dates from the end of the seventeenth century, and more or less completely replaces an earlier manor house, was built for William Blathwayt, a diplomat and Secretary of State to William III. The fine decoration and contents owe much to Blathwayt's close links with the Netherlands and the American colonies. In the formal grounds are the remains of an elaborate water garden, now marked only by a rather solitary statue of Neptune.

MAIN PICTURE: THE MASSIVE RAMPARTS OF DOLEBURY HILLFORT. RIGHT: DYRHAM PARK.

THE GEORGE INN

The George Inn, situated in the old wool village of Norton St. Philip in Somerset, is sometimes held to be the oldest inn in the country. Such a claim is impossible to prove of course, but it certainly looks the part with its stone-built ground floor and two later timber-frame upper storeys. A flower-filled courtyard and long medieval gallery complete the picturesque effect. Among its notable visitors have been Samuel Pepys and the Duke of Monmouth, who made it his headquarters in 1685 after retreating from Bath.

FOREST OF DEAN

The Forest of Dean, with its unique atmosphere and independent character, is one of the most beautiful stretches of forest land in the country. This has much to do with its geographical location: bounded on each side by a river—the Wye to the west and the Severn to the east—it has preserved a way of life, set of customs and a topography that are very different from the surrounding countryside.

The forest's natural resources have been ruthlessly exploited since the Romans mined iron ore in great surface excavations throughout the area. For centuries after that, the forest provided timber for iron forges and the navy's massive shipbuilding programmes. Coal mining was a further encroachment on the land and continues to this day. A number of quaintly-named pits attest to the activities of the forest's Free Miners, who have worked the forest's seams since the fourteenth century. As well as their traditional mineral rights, the residents of the forest still have grazing rights over a larger area than anywhere else in the country.

The forest today is very much the work of its present custodians, the Forestry Commission, who have been planting and managing it since 1924. There are many lovely walks and trails through the woodlands and hills, and a recent project has introduced contemporary sculpture specially commissioned for sites in the forest.

There are several attractive little towns in the area, including the busy market town of Coleford, and Lydney which has been a thriving little port since the Romans used it for the transportation of their iron ore.

HORTON COURT

Horton Court is a lovely example of a Cotswold manor house, with a fascinating history somewhat belying its archetypally English appearance. The estate was given in 1125 to the cathedral at Salisbury; it was a valuable addition to the property of the diocese and was owned by a succession of senior ecclesiastics. The Norman Hall, built in about 1140, survives from that time, and is now the north wing of the house.

Most of the rest of the house as it now stands was built in 1521 for William Knight, the prebendary of Horton from 1517 who later became Bishop of Bath and Wells. He was much influenced by a period spent in Italy studying law as a young man, and the house reflected his fascination with Italian style. Renaissance arabesques decorate the magnificent front door, and a Renaissance frieze and classical pilasters adorn the Tudor fireplace, while the famous ambulatory in the garden incorporates the stucco heads of a gallery of Roman emperors.

The front door also bears Knight's own coat-of-arms—fabricated, apparently, since he was of fairly humble birth. It is a masterpiece of compromise, or perhaps diplomacy: the rose of Lancaster, the sun of York and the eagle of the Holy Roman Emperor Charles V.

MAIN PICTURE: THE FOREST OF DEAN. RIGHT: THE ANCIENT GEORGE INN. BOTTOM: HORTON COURT.

GLASTONBURY

It is almost impossible to divorce present-day Glastonbury from the mist of myth and legend that has grown up around the town over the centuries—even the street-names on the modern housing estates on the outskirts hark back to the folklore of Arthurian England. The name Glastonbury immediately brings to mind an image that is familiar from countless photographs, illustrations and paintings: that of the Glastonbury Tor, topped by St. Michael's Tower. Rising from the flat land of the North Somerset Levels, it more often than not emerges from the mists of the plain like the magical monument it is held to be.

The Glastonbury legends tell of Christ coming here as a child with his uncle, Joseph of Arimathea, who later returned and hid the Holy Grail under a spring on the spot now known as Chalice Well. The Glastonbury Thorn, it is said, grew from the place where Joseph rested his staff on the ground; it flowers every Christmas, and a sprig is still sent each year at this time to the Queen.

Legend also has it that Glastonbury is the site of the Isle of Avalon, and that King Arthur and Queen Guinevere are buried in the Abbey graveyard. There are, however, grounds for suspecting that this belief originates from a pragmatic piece of myth-making on the part of the medieval monks who found themselves in dire need of funds when rebuilding their abbey. It almost does not matter where the truth lies; what is undeniable is that Glastonbury has played such an evocative role in English legend that the place is steeped in a special magic of its own.

Glastonbury's importance in the past rested on the pre-eminence of its religious order, which by the time of Domesday was the most powerful in Somerset. An enormous abbey and surrounding monastic buildings were established in the eleventh and twelfth centuries, but burnt down almost totally in 1184. Rebuilding began immediately—helped by the discovery of King Arthur's grave—and a magnificent new abbey was created, with cloisters and domestic buildings. It continued to thrive until the Dissolution of the Monasteries in the sixteenth century, when its last abbot was beheaded and his head impaled on the abbey gate. The building was then plundered and used as a quarry for several hundred years, although the Abbot's Kitchen survived, and now includes an exhibition outlining the history of the abbey.

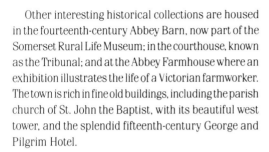

Other interesting historical collections are housed in the fourteenth-century Abbey Barn, now part of the Somerset Rural Life Museum; in the courthouse, known as the Tribunal; and at the Abbey Farmhouse where an exhibition illustrates the life of a Victorian farmworker. The town is rich in fine old buildings, including the parish church of St. John the Baptist, with its beautiful west tower, and the splendid fifteenth-century George and Pilgrim Hotel.

KENNET AND AVON CANAL

The Kennet and Avon Canal was built in 1810 and runs between Bath and Reading. Linking Bristol with the rest of the national canal network, it was a spectacular piece of industrial engineering in its time, and has recently been the subject of intensive restoration work.

The most impressive stretch of all, in terms of the sheer magnitude of its construction, covers two miles up Caen Hill, west of Devizes. Here 29 locks—the longest flight of locks in Britain—raise the canal by 230 ft. (70 m.).

Like many of Britain's canals, it fell into gradual disuse in the course of the nineteenth century in the face of competition from the railways.

The task of restoration has been enormous, and the canal has gradually come back into use section by section through the efforts of the Kennet and Avon Canal Trust. The entire length of its 87-mile towpath is a public right-of-way, providing a wonderful long-distance walk through some of Southern England's most peaceful and attractive scenery. A number of locks are particularly picturesque, and there is nothing more pleasant on a summer's evening than to sit at one of the waterside pubs on the canal and watch the river traffic go by.

The history and story of the restoration of the canal are given in a fascinating exhibition at the canal Centre in Devizes.

TOP: THE DRAMATIC RUINS OF GLASTONBURY ABBEY. BOTTOM: GLASTONBURY TOR. RIGHT: PEWSEY WHARF ON THE KENNET AND AVON CANAL.

LACOCK

Lacock in Wiltshire is packed with delights—architectural, photographic and gastronomic. The entire village and the abbey have been owned by the National Trust since 1944, and their renovation as a tourist attraction has been sensitively managed.

The village streets running off the wide High Street are lined with timber-frame and stone buildings, most of which date from between 1300 and 1800. Among them are a number of fine old inns serving excellent food. Many of the houses are former weavers' cottages built during the time when the wool trade supported this and many other villages in the area.

Lacock Abbey was originally a thirteenth-century nunnery, and still retains its medieval cloisters, sacristy

and chapter house. It was converted to a private home in 1540, and then much remodelled in the eighteenth-century Gothic style for the Talbot family who owned it by then. One of the oriel windows of the house became the subject of the first-known photograph, taken in 1835 by William Henry Fox Talbot, the local M.P. and pioneer of photography. His photographic equipment and early experiments in photography, many of which took place in and around Lacock, are displayed in the nearby Fox Talbot Museum, which is housed in an old tithe barn by the Abbey Gate.

LECHLADE

Lechlade takes its name from the River Leach, which runs through one of the Cotswolds' fertile river valleys into the Thames a few fields away. Once famous for its commercial river trade, the town now has a small marina and is a great centre for holiday boat traffic.

In the centre of town is the market place with its great 'wool church' of St. Lawrence, one of the churches endowed by the wealthy merchants who made their fortunes from the Cotswold wool and cloth trade. Its atmospheric churchyard inspired Shelley to write his 'Stanzas in Lechlade Churchyard' in 1815.

The thirteenth-century stone-floored Trout Inn is one of several excellent pubs in the town. There is also a trout farm at nearby Farringdon Mill—the site of a working mill from the time of Domesday Book until only a few years ago.

LONGLEAT

Longleat House in Wiltshire, the family seat of the Marquess of Bath, was the first 'stately home' in Britain to open to the public as a commercial proposition. This was in 1949, and since then it has exploited its commercial potential energetically, becoming a hugely popular tourist attraction, both for the splendour of the house itself and for its famous Safari Park.

The house is superbly situated in beautiful grounds on the site of a thirteenth-century Augustinian priory. It was built in the 1570s for Sir John Thynne, an ancestor of the present owner, who had bought the estate from the Crown in 1540 for £53. All the façades of the four-square house are similar, their tall Elizabethan mullioned windows topped by a flamboyant roofline featuring balustrades and stone figurines. The house is enormous, with over a hundred rooms. Of those that are open to the public, many are gorgeously decorated with ornate moulded ceilings, sumptuous furnishings and fine paintings, including an excellent gallery of Elizabethan portraits. It would be difficult to single out any one particular room for special attention, as there are so many which vie in magnificence. This is the English aristocratic heritage at its most opulent.

The gardens—little changed from the time when they were landscaped in 1757 by Capability Brown, who also designed the stable block and orangery—contain a number of visitor attractions. A large adventure

MAIN PICTURE: RIVER LEACH AT LECHLADE. LEFT: LACOCK. RIGHT: LONGLEAT HOUSE.

playground for children, a miniature railway and the world's largest maze are among the most popular features.

Many visitors to Longleat are drawn not so much by the attractions of one of Britain's most impressive stately homes as by the justifiably famous Safari Park. This park, the first outside Africa, was opened in 1966, and a trip around the 100-acre reserve is a really memorable experience. Visitors can either drive their cars or take a special Safari bus through a series of enclosures where tigers, lions and many other animals roam freely, often approaching within feet of the vehicles or, in the case of cheekier creatures like the monkeys, landing on top of them. There are lakes where boats take visitors out to see hippopotamuses and sealions, a gorilla island, and a pets' corner for children.

To add to its already numerous attractions, Longleat has the country's only permanent 'Dr Who' exhibition, based on the popular BBC children's series.

THE MENDIPS

The Mendip Hills lie south of Bristol, forming a dramatic divide between the counties of Avon and Somerset. The limestone ridge runs for 20 miles from Frome in Somerset to the coast, and drops sharply on its south slopes to the great flat stretch of the Somerset Levels. The western end of the hills has been declared an area of outstanding natural beauty, not only for the often spectacular landscape to be enjoyed above ground, but also for the rarer attractions of the underground caves and caverns with which the hills are honeycombed.

These caves contain traces of man's earliest history in the region. Fossil remains of prehistoric mammals like bison, reindeer, bears and wolves tell of a time before the land was settled, while caves at Cheddar, Westbury and Wookey have revealed flints and remains of prehistoric man.

Mendip is a beautiful place for walking and rambling and is renowned for beauty spots like Cheddar, but it also has a long industrial history. This goes back to the time of the Romans, who mined the hills extensively for lead, particularly at Charterhouse in the west. Stone has been quarried from Mendip since the Middle Ages, and quarry trucks still rumble over the hills every day.

Priddy, the only town on the top of Mendip, has been at the centre of human and industrial activity since prehistoric man built the barrows and stone circles that can be seen outside the town today. It was a lead-mining centre for the Romans, and became a great market

centre in the Middle Ages when Mendip sheep grew wool for the lucrative cloth-making trade in the valleys. Sheep trading still continues at Priddy, its significance marked by the pile of sheep hurdles on the green, no longer used themselves but a symbol of the centuries-old trade. The annual Priddy Fair in August is still an important date in the regional farming calendar, and one which marks Mendip's continuing role in the local economy.

MONTACUTE HOUSE

Montacute House, now in the hands of the National Trust, is one of the earliest and very best examples of an Elizabethan mansion house. Built of honey-coloured stone from the local quarry of Ham Hill, and characterised by the large windows so much loved by the Elizabethans, it is an outstanding piece of Renaissance architecture: grand, and yet not intimidating, and surrounded by beautiful gardens.

The house was built by Somerset landowner and speaker of the House of Commons, Sir Edward Phelips, at the very end of the sixteenth century, the date (1601) carved above the east doorway probably marking its completion. Sir Edward collaborated with a talented local stonemason, William Arnold, whose hand is best appreciated on the east façade—the original front of the house—which is gloriously decorated with bays, cornices, columns, obelisks and statues. In front of the

east façade is a formal garden, flanked by two delicate domed gazebos, which, with the ornamental gardens on the north and south fronts, creates a beautifully simple and thoroughly effective setting for the mansion. The house is now approached by the west front, created in the late eighteenth century by another Edward Phelips, who bought the porch and other ornamental features from Clifton Maybank, a Tudor house in Dorset, and fitted them into the west wing of Montacute.

The inside of the house has remained almost unchanged, and now contains, in the restored 172 ft. Long Gallery, a superb collection of paintings on loan from the National Portrait Gallery. Tudor and Jacobean portraits gaze from the walls with faces that belong utterly to the spirit of the place—fitting treasures for an almost perfect Elizabethan relic.

MAIN PICTURE: CROOKS PEAK, THE HIGHEST POINT OF THE MENDIPS. BOTTOM RIGHT: MONTACUTE HOUSE.

119

SLIMBRIDGE

Slimbridge in Gloucestershire is the headquarters of the Wildfowl Trust, home of the world's largest and most varied collection of wildfowl. The Trust, founded by naturalist Sir Peter Scott, has six other reserves in Britain, and works to protect wildfowl threatened with extinction and to encourage people to observe and enjoy birds in their natural environment.

At Slimbridge there are over 180 different kinds of birds, ranging from rare visiting geese and swans to tiny humming birds in the Tropical House and elegant flocks of flamingos which wander the landscaped gardens.

THE RIDGEWAY

The Ridgeway is a prehistoric highway running through Wiltshire, up across the Oxfordshire and Berkshire Downs, and on into Buckinghamshire. From the Wiltshire village of Avebury it is a designated long-distance footpath, and is excellent walking territory, whether for short outings or longer expeditions. In places the track is up to 40 ft. wide and lined with ancient hedgerows, and there are wonderful views to be enjoyed along its whole length.

There are many points of archaeological interest along the way, including a white horse on Hackpen Hill near Marlborough. One of a number of such hill carvings in Wiltshire, the Broad Hinton White Horse is 90 ft. long and 90 ft. high, and was carved in 1838, apparently to commemorate the coronation of Queen Victoria.

The route of the Ridgeway passes near two well-defined Iron Age hillforts: Barbury Castle, where weapons, tools and chariot equipment have been found, and Liddington Castle, said to be the site of King Arthur's victory over the Saxons at Mons Badonicus.

SALTFORD AND THE AVON VALLEY

Saltford lies in the Avon Valley between Bristol and Bath, and takes its name from the old ford across the river which is still identifiable on the south side of Kelston Bridge in the village. Despite its obvious attraction for commuters from both cities, it still has the feel of a small, intimate village community, with its Norman church and manor-house, and its cottage-lined High Street.

The busy little marina at Saltford indicates how much leisure-boat traffic there is on this stretch of river, and the whole of the Avon valley has become very popular for leisure activities of all kinds. The Saltford Regatta was once a high spot of the summer, with great crowds lining the river banks; today they have been replaced by picnickers, walkers and anglers, drawn by the irresistible combination of messing around on the river and relaxing in the countryside. The demise of the Midland Railway line between Bristol and Bath has been turned to the advantage of cyclists and walkers, who can enjoy the recently-created path along the old track. A number of excellent riverside pubs add to the area's appeal, the most popular being the Jolly Sailor Inn, once a favourite stop for bargemen and now well-patronised by visitors.

Viewing towers and hides on the reserve allow visitors to observe normally shy birds at close quarters, and a recently-built swan observatory provides a perfect vantage point over the famous Swan Lake. Nature trails around the reserve are specially designed to help visitors identify all the bird species, as well as providing very pleasant walks through the reserve's 800 acres.

Slimbridge is a perfect place to introduce children to wildlife, particularly in the spring and summer when young ducklings, goslings and cygnets roam the grounds.

TOP: THE RIDGEWAY NEAR THE A4 AT AVEBURY. RIGHT: SLIMBRIDGE WILDFOWL TRUST. CENTRE BOTTOM: THE JOLLY SAILOR INN AT SALTFORD.

STONEHENGE

Stonehenge in Wiltshire is one of the most important prehistoric monuments in the world, and, despite intense speculation and research, remains one of the most enigmatic and mysterious. Religious, astronomical or sacrificial, the origins of these huge standing stones may never be revealed; despite advances in archaeology, the monument continues to defy categorisation.

Constructed on a vast scale, the site was quite clearly one of great significance to its neolithic builders, who would have had to transport the stones many miles from at least two different sources. The enormous sarsen stones probably came from the Marlborough Downs to the north, and must have been dragged overland. The smaller bluestones of the inner circles (still weighing up to four tons, nonetheless) appear to have come from Pembrokeshire in South Wales, and could have been transported by water for much of the journey.

The monument was built in three phases, the first between 3000 and 2500 B.C. when the ditch and bank were developed. It is believed that the massive stone circles were then created in stages over a 1,000-year period.

The axis of the monument, with the central heelstone or altar stone in the middle, lies along the line of the first rays of the sun on Midsummer Day, leading to speculation that it served as a gigantic calendar or prehistoric astronomical observatory. The Victorians, with their ghoulish fascination for the macabre, thought it was a Druid centre for human sacrifice. Celebrants of Druid rituals have gathered there for many years, recently joined by more modern pilgrims in the form of convoys of hippies and 'travellers', who have adopted it as a symbol of a golden age of peace and harmony, rather to the distress of some local residents.

Stonehenge's immense fascination for visitors is certainly both a blessing and a curse for its custodians, the Department of the Environment, who have had to take measures to safeguard the stones from the wear and tear of constant sightseers. The image of the massive stones against an overarching sky has a firm hold on the popular imagination and never fails to impress first-time visitors—all the more so for the continuing mystery of its origins.

Stow-on-the-Wold, 'where the wind blows cold', is perched 800 ft. up on the top of an exposed hill. It is perhaps one of the best-known Cotswold towns, partly because of its location at the crossing of several important roads, including the nearby Roman Fosse Way. It is still a crossroads and stopping-off point for visitors, many of whom take advantage of its renowned tea shops to take a welcome break on what is often a whistlestop tour around the Cotswolds.

The size of its market square testifies to its former pre-eminence as a centre for trade. When the Cotswolds became rich from the wool and cloth industry, Stow's two annual sheep and cattle fairs were great occasions both in terms of the local economy and for their importance in the social calendar. Another reminder of the square's former function is the original town stocks, still to be seen at one end.

The church was used for Royalist prisoners after the Battle of Donnington in the Civil War, after which it was declared ruined, but later restored.

STOURHEAD

Stourhead is perhaps the most glorious and perfect example of eighteenth-century garden landscaping in the country. Situated at the headwaters of the river Stour, next to the little village of Stourton, the house and gardens are now owned by the National Trust and are one of the 'jewels in its crown'.

The gardens were created between 1741 and 1785 by the estate's owner, Henry Hoare II, around a magnificent lake formed by the damming of the river. Their original design remains more or less unaltered, and indeed the gardens we see today are probably even more beautiful in their maturity than they were two and a half centuries ago. They were planned to provide a series of splendid vistas across the lake from vantage points at its edge and on the slopes around it. A number of classical buildings and appealingly idiosyncratic features are carefully placed to enhance the effect. Various Greek temples represent the eighteenth-century ideal of classical harmony between architecture and landscape, while lakeside grottoes (complete with

statues), tumbling waterfalls and occasional rustic cottages show the inspiration of an early Romantic sensibility. A magnificent collection of trees and shrubs superbly laid out is evidence of a truly inspired landscape gardener. Spring and early summer, when the displays of azaleas and rhododendrons are nothing short of spectacular, are the very best times to visit the gardens, but there really is no bad time for a visit to Stourhead. One other notable feature of the gardens is the fourteenth-century Bristol High Cross, given to Stourhead in 1765 by Bristol corporation, which was anxious to find a safe haven for it in the face of moves to demolish it. There it has remained ever since, peculiarly at home in its unlikely surroundings.

The house was built in 1721 for Henry Hoare's father in the Palladian style, the two wings being added in about 1800 for Richard Colt Hoare, the noted Wiltshire historian. Much of the house was rebuilt after being gutted by fire in 1902, but the splendid library and the picture gallery survived unscathed. There are fine collections of pictures and sculpture in the house, as well as furniture by Chippendale the Younger.

MAIN PICTURE: STOURHEAD GARDENS. TOP RIGHT: STOW-ON-THE-WOLD. BOTTOM RIGHT: THE PICTURESQUE COTSWOLD VILLAGE OF LOWER SLAUGHTER, JUST A FEW MILES FROM STOW-ON-THE-WOLD.

TETBURY

Tetbury's large market hall—once even more impressive than it is now—is an indication of how important the town was as a trading centre during the great days of the Cotswold woollen industry. Its prosperity continued after the general collapse of this trade, partly perhaps because the townspeople had had the foresight to buy the manor from Lord Berkeley in the early seventeenth century and run it themselves.

The streets that lead off the market place contain many fine seventeenth- and eighteenth-century Cotswold-stone houses. The church of St. Mary dates from 1781 and contains an interesting collection of large monuments. The later St. Saviour's was apparently built to accommodate the poor who could not find pews in St. Mary's once the town's wealthy merchants had endowed—that is to say *bought*—them all.

TINTERN ABBEY

Tintern Abbey stands, roofless and windowless, on lush meadowland beside the River Wye—a magnificent ruin. It was the high spot of the eighteenth-century Wye tour, a monument of 'awful grandeur' in the words of one poet, despite the adjoining hovels and the crowds of beggars who used to congregate there to accost the picnicking tourists. The hovels have long since disappeared, and the crowds are now sightseers rather than beggars, but the effect of the abbey is little changed.

It was founded in 1131 for the Cistercians, a Benedictine sect who had established their first 'House' in England only three years previously. The present ruins are of a building which replaced the original abbey in the thirteenth century, by which time the order was

extremely wealthy and powerful, with land on both sides of the river and further afield. Like similar religious buildings throughout the country, Tintern Abbey was stripped of its wealth during Henry VIII's Dissolution of the Monasteries. The land was sold, the bells and lead were removed, the abbot was pensioned off and the building fell into ruins. After the dissolution, the abbey and surrounding lands were granted to the Earl of Worcester, whose family later became the Dukes of Beaufort, and it remained in their possession until it was sold to the Crown in 1901.

The Department of the Environment has carried out a good deal of cleaning and restoration work on the abbey, removing in the process the picturesque but pernicious ivy that so appealed to the visiting Romantic poets, and adding such contemporary essentials as a car park and café. Modern tourist amenities notwithstanding, it is impossible to walk through the ruins of the massive Abbey Church and gaze out of the huge, empty East Window without sensing the grandeur that still clings to the building.

WEST SOMERSET RAILWAY

The West Somerset Railway is Britain's longest privately-owned line. It was opened in 1976, having closed five years previously as a public line, and runs from Bishop's Lydeard near Taunton to Minehead on the Somerset coast. The railway is run by a small

permanent staff and a large body of enthusiastic volunteers, who help keep in year-round operation five diesel locomotives. Five steam engines provide an added summer attraction. There are eight stops along the 20-mile line, which runs through very pretty Somerset countryside, and views of the Quantock and Brendon Hills are plentiful before the journey ends at the sea. At Watchet, the oldest commercial harbour in Somerset, the track approaches within metres of the shore, and then runs along the coast through the 'fairy-tale' village of Dunster, with its castle on the hillside, and on to the popular seaside resort of Minehead.

TOP LEFT: TETBURY MARKET PLACE. TOP RIGHT: TINTERN ABBEY. BOTTOM RIGHT: WILLITON STATION ON THE WEST SOMERSET RAILWAY.

123

WELLS

Wells is England's smallest city, and is famous for one of her most beautiful cathedrals. But it is not only this superb Gothic monument that lends Wells a particular charm: the city has an extraordinarily rich heritage of religious architecture that survives remarkably intact. Somehow, despite many thousands of visitors and the attendant traffic problems, and whilst maintaining a bustling commercial life in its own right, Wells has managed to keep at its heart a sense of space and quietude that is rarely to be found in larger cathedral cities.

The city takes its name from the natural springs which bubble in the bottom of a pool, now situated in the Bishop's Garden, whose waters run through the gutters in the High Street. A Saxon church founded near these wells was eventually superseded by the present cathedral. Building commenced in 1180, and work on the magnificent West Front began about 50 years later. It carries over 290 pieces of medieval sculpture across the façade—quite the most extraordinary collection, and one which has been the object of dedicated restoration work. Inside, the cathedral is a supreme example of the Early English Gothic style, its austere simplicity relieved by the exuberance of the carved

MAIN PICTURE: WELLS CATHEDRAL. BOTTOM: THE FORTIFIED
BISHOP'S PALACE.

gures around its pillars and the beautiful stained glass at its East End.

Among many fine features of the cathedral, probably the best known is the astronomical clock, which has a seated figure striking each quarter while four knights on horseback enact a tournament.

From the North Transept a well-worn and much-photographed flight of steps leads up to the thirteenth-century Chapter House, from where a covered bridge leads to Vicars' Close. This is the oldest complete medieval street in Europe, dating back in part to the fourteenth century. Nearby is the Old Deanery, a fine fifteenth-century house now used as the diocesan offices, and next to it the Wells Museum in the old Chancellor's House.

On the other side of the cathedral, surrounded by graceful gardens and a picturesque moat, is the Bishop's Palace, the residence of the bishops of Bath and Wells for over 700 years.

There is far more to Wells than this impressive group of medieval church buildings: it was the largest town in Somerset until exceeded by Bath in the eighteenth century, and there are many indications of its years of importance. The thirteenth-century parish church of St. Cuthbert, whose splendid tower is often mistaken for the cathedral by first-time visitors, marked the centre of the city's trade until the Market Place grew up next to the cathedral in the fifteenth century. In the Market Place today, as a sign that Wells is not content merely to rest on its medieval laurels, a marker on the pavement measures out the Olympic long-jumping record established in 1964 by Wells-born athlete Mary Rand.

WESTON-SUPER-MARE

Weston-super-Mare is the chief seaside resort within easy reach of Bristol, and attracts three million visitors a year from all over the country. It became popular in the nineteenth century, growing from a tiny fishing village with a population of 163 in 1811 to the second largest town in Somerset a hundred years later, an expansion much encouraged by the arrival of the railway in 1841.

Early holidaymakers included many who went for their health, the climate being highly recommended by medical experts. In addition to its bracing air, still an attraction for convalescents, its two miles of sandy beaches make it a perfect family resort, and there are enough seaside amusements to provide entertainment for all constitutions and all ages.

Two piers, a marine lake, a miniature railway on beach lawns, an aquarium and the recently opened Tropicana pleasure beach and surf pool—'Fun, Fruity, Wet and Wild'—guarantee amusement even when the weather is less than perfect. The town has attractive parks and gardens, two theatres, the Winter Gardens' ballroom, many pubs and clubs for evening entertainment, and a delightful museum.

If the appeal of this busy resort begins to pale, the surrounding coast and countryside offer many walks and quiet beauty spots well off the tourist track.

WESTONBIRT

The village of Westonbirt in Gloucestershire is famous for its arboretum, which boasts an exceptional collection of trees in its 250 acres. The main attractions are the spring-flowering trees and shrubs such as azaleas and rhododendrons, and the spectacular blaze of reds and golds in autumn. It is nevertheless well worth a visit at any time of year for the sheer pleasure afforded by the surroundings, and, for a better appreciation of the displays, visitors are encouraged to leave the footpaths and wander amongst the trees.

TOP LEFT: VICARS' CLOSE, WELLS. RIGHT: WESTON-SUPER-MARE.
BOTTOM: WESTONBIRT ARBORETUM.

WOOKEY HOLE

Wookey Hole, two miles north of Wells, is where the River Axe emerges from its underground course through the Mendips. Its Great Cave, hung with stalactites, has been a tourist attraction since at least the fifteenth century, and is one of Mendip's most spectacular underground treasures. The caves have provided evidence of early human habitation in the shape of pottery, weaving equipment and coins from as early as 250 B.C. Even more exciting are the Palaeolithic human and animal remains dating back as far as 50000 B.C. which were found in the adjoining Hyena Den, so called because most of the animal bones were thought to have been chewed by the hyenas who shared the caves with Palaeolithic man. Today, the most famous inhabitant of Wookey Hole is the Witch of Wookey, who was turned to stone, legend has it, by a brave monk from Glastonbury.

Paper has been made at a mill at Wookey, using the power of the River Axe, since at least the seventeenth century. Mill and caves were bought by Madame Tussaud's in 1973, and as well as producing fine hand-made paper again, part of the mill has become a store and studio for the famous waxworks museum. Also on show is a wonderful collection of fairground objects.

THE WYE VALLEY

The Wye Valley is an area of great, and occasionally spectacular, beauty, forming a natural if not geographically precise boundary between England and Wales. Its steep wooden slopes, rocky outcrops and gently meandering river were much appreciated by eighteenth- and nineteenth-century writers and painters looking for the sublime in nature. Wordsworth's 'Lines Written a Few Miles Above Tintern Abbey' perfectly capture the appeal of the Wye Valley for these early Romantics.

Long before the Wye Tour became an eighteenth century attraction, the river was a busy trading artery with a thriving traffic of goods and raw materials to and from Bristol. The advent of the railway killed off the commercial river traffic, but increased the tourist trade. Now that the railway has in turn closed down, the traffic is by road, and often very heavy in high tourist season. Despite its popularity, the valley is still the place of tranquil and inspiring beauty that so attracted its eighteenth-century visitors. Spots like Tintern Abbey and Symonds Yat are inevitably crowded, but there are many miles of woodland and riverside walks, and magnificent hilltop views to be enjoyed—far from the crowds.

TOP LEFT: WOOKEY HOLE. TOP RIGHT: FERRY ACROSS THE WYE AT SYMONDS YAT. MAIN PICTURE: WYE VALLEY VIEWED FROM THE FORESTRY COMMISSION VIEWPOINT AT SYMONDS YAT ROCK.

INDEX OF HEADINGS

ACKNOWLEDGEMENTS

Additional text by the City Museum and Art Gallery and the Press and Public Relations Office.

Photographs by the Exhibition and Graphic Design Section of the City Planning Department.

Cover photograph by John Chalcraft.

Additional photographs: Plasmaglobe (page 54) by Martin Haswell, supplied by the Exploratory. Video training (page 72) supplied by the Watershed. Courage Brewery (page 87) by Cotters Photography, supplied by Courage's (Western) Ltd. American Museum (page 108) supplied by the American Museum. Dyrham Park (page 115) supplied by the National Trust. Longleat House (page 118) supplied by Longleat House. Montacute House (page 119) supplied by the National Trust. Stourhead (page 122) by John Chalcraft. West Somerset Railway (page 123) by T. A. Clift. Weston-super-Mare (page 125) supplied by the District of Woodspring. Wookey Hole (page 126) supplied by Wookey Hole Caves Ltd.

Archive photographs and other illustrations: drawing by Pocock (page 3) from the log of the *Lloyd*, Bristol Record Office. Medieval seal (page 14), Bristol Record Office. Photograph of St. Augustine's Reach in 1865 (page 20), City Museum and Art Gallery. The Mayors Calendar (page 29), Bristol Record Office. Sir George Oatley's design for the Wills Memorial Building (page 39), University of Bristol. *Death of Chatterton* by H. Wallis (page 52), Tate Gallery, London. Photograph of the Phoenix Glass Kiln (page 52), City Museum and Art Gallery. Bristol Old Station (page 53) lithograph by J. C. Bourne. Bristol Bridge from Millerd's map of 1673 (page 86), City Museum and Art Gallery. *Illustrated London News* (page 90), City Museum and Art Gallery. Early bridge proposal and Clifton Spa (page 91), City Museum and Art Gallery.

Research information supplied by Bristol City Council Record Office.

Assistance with reading and proof checking by the City Museum and Art Gallery and the Record Office. Editorial assistance and Index compilation by the Printing and Stationery Department.

BIBLIOGRAPHY

Ashton Court Mansion—Historic Development and Future Potential
(Bristol City Council, 1987).
Aspects of Railway Architecture
(British Rail/Bristol City Council, 1984).
Bristol: An Architectural History
A. Gomme, M. Jenner, B. Little (Lund Humphries in association with the Bristol and West Building Society, 1979).
The Bristol Book
(Bristol City Council, 1983).
Bristol Cathedral
(English Life Publications, 1984).
Bristol Curiosities
R. Winstone, G. Duggan (Redcliffe Press, 1979).
The Bristol Hippodrome: A Souvenir of 75 Years
(Proscenium Publications, 1987).
Bristol—Official Visitors' Guide
(Bristol City Council, 1986 edition).
Bristol Zoo Gardens
(Bristol, Clifton and West of England Zoological Society, 1987).
Companion into Gloucestershire and the Cotswolds
R. P. Beckinsale (Spurbooks Ltd., 1973).
Excavations at St. Bartholomew's Hospital, Bristol
R. Price, City of Bristol Museum (Redcliffe Press, 1979).
The Great Western Railway 1835–1985
(G.W.R. 150/Bristol Marketing Board, 1985).
A Guide to Bristol Building Trust Initiatives in Bristol
(Bristol Buildings Preservation Trust).
The National Trust Book of Great Houses of Britain
N. Nicolson (Book Club Associates by arrangement with Weidenfeld & Nicholson and the National Trust, 1978).
Notes on the History of St. Mary's-on-the-Quay
M. Fedden (Burleigh Press).
Portrait of Avon
J. Haddon (Robert Hale, 1981).
Portrait of Wiltshire
P. Street (Robert Hale, 1973).
The Problems of Consolidation in the Bristol Flint Glass Industry
C. Weeden (from Glass Technology Vol. 22 No. 5, 5.10.81).
Redcliffe Caves
T. Bisgrove (article—'Adrian's Mole', Bristol City Council, 1987).
The River Wye
K. Kissack (Terence Dalton Ltd., 1978).
The Ricketts Family and the Phoenix Glasshouse, Bristol
C. Weeden (from The Glass Circle, December 1982).
Somerset and Avon
R. Dunning (John Bartholomew and Son Ltd., 1980).
St. Mark's: The Lord Mayor's Chapel in Bristol
E. Ralph and H. Evans (City of Bristol, 1979).
A University for Bristol
D. Carleton (University of Bristol Press, 1984).
Village England
ed. P. Crookston (Book Club Associates in association with Hutchinson & Co., 1980).
A Visitor's Guide to the Cotswolds
R. Sale (1982).
The West Country
B. Le. Messurier (Regional Guides to Britain, Ward Lock Ltd., 1982).
Wiltshire
M. Child (Shire County Guides, Shire Publications, 1984).
The Wye Valley
E. J. Mason (Robert Hale Ltd., 1987).

A BRISTOL TRAM OF THE 1930s.